THE FILM BIZ BIBLE

THE INDEPENDENT FILM BUSINESS

THE FILM BIZ BIBLE

THE INDEPENDENT FILM BUSINESS

ANSWERS TO QUESTIONS YOU DID NOT EVEN KNOW TO ASK!

A PRACTICAL GUIDE TO THE REAL WORLD OF

INDEPENDENT FILM PRODUCING, FILM FINANCING,

SELLING, MARKETING & DISTRIBUTION

OF INDEPENDENT FEATURE FILMS, FROM A

HOLLYWOOD INSIDER WITH OVER 25 YEARS

IN THE INDEPENDENT FILM BUSINESS.

WRITTEN BY JOHN RODSETT

Published by: FILM BIZ SEMINAR INC.
Corporate address: 542 N. 5th Avenue, Sequim, WA 98382

Library Of Congress Cataloging-in-publication
John Rodsett
THE FILM BIZ BIBLE/John Rodsett
ISBN-13: 978-1452893976
ISBN-10: 1452893977

For information on all Film Biz Seminar Inc.
publications, seminars, webinars, film activities
visit: www.mrfilmbiz.com

Printed in the United States of America

"THE FILM BIZ BIBLE"
THE INDEPENDENT FILM BUSINESS

INTRODUCTION

This book is written for the sole purpose of helping independent filmmakers, actors, directors, producers and anyone interested in the "indie" film world, to have a comprehensive insider's view of many of the business aspects of the independent film world. It is a practical interpretation of many topics and issues confronting today's filmmakers and hopefully it will offer insight and potential solutions to the many complex decisions and strategies.

This book is <u>not</u> a text book (as most books on the film business are) and it is not a comprehensive guide to every aspect of the film universe. This book is written in a unique blog style format, specifically covering independent film industry <u>business</u> topics that I want filmmakers, writers, directors and producers to focus on.

After twenty five years being in the film industry, I wanted to "give back" to the film community by providing a two day independent film business seminar (www.mrfilmbiz.com) and this book. The book is a companion supplement to the seminar and provides enhanced coverage of many of the topics covered in my two day seminar.

I have truly lived it, done it, made movies, sold films and made money in the independent film industry for many years... How unique is that!! I hope you can learn from a producer/sales agent/deal maker with nearly three decades in the independent feature film industry.

This comprehensive Hollywood insider's view of the business aspects of the independent feature film industry offers solutions, insightful, practical answers and advice on the complex topics and decisions that will affect you in your own independent film career path.

- How do you fund a film?
- How do you find investors?...Once you find them, how do you close the deal?
- You want to sell your own film in today's marketplace – Do you have any idea where to start?
- You want to understand the film business?

This book and the two day seminar provide you with the knowledge and tools to excel, to create your own success in this film industry.

Topics covered will provide clear, concise, practical advice and knowledge that will help guide readers through a film business that is very complex, constantly evolving, yet many of the principles of the business remain the same and have done for many years.

In the film industry, ignorance is not bliss, and in many instances can cause abject failure and the destruction of the dreams of aspiring filmmakers. I want this book to help give tips, advice and clarity on important film business topics that will help you in your film ventures.

I am a man of very few written words, but I can talk to individuals or audiences all day long about the independent feature film industry. I love this film business and it has given me a fabulous life for over thirty years. From my early days at 20th Century Fox, through the video boom years of the late 1980's and most of the 1990's and then through my last decade of my consulting on films, event sponsorship and to being a full time adjunct professor at major universities in the USA.

This book came about from the fact that I have taught university classes about the motion picture industry. I have interacted with many aspiring independent filmmakers, actors, writers, producers over many years and certain glaring consistencies keep coming up that need addressing. These consistencies are all about filmmaking and the business aspects of the independent film business that in one way or another, either through ignorance, lack of knowledge or just lack of common sense, cause filmmakers to fall short of their dreams and aspirations. I am a Hollywood insider turned professor for the benefit of you, the filmmaker!

This is a compilation of many thoughts and topics written in a clear, direct and practical way. I hope that readers will be able to use the information I impart, as tools to assist in attaining their goals, based on my knowledge and experience of having done this business for many, many years.

Believe me, everything in this book I have experienced myself – the good, the bad and the ugly! It is from those experiences gained over many years in the trenches of independent film making, development, producing, financing, production, marketing, selling and distribution I give you this book.

I have sectioned the book into major topic categories, similar to my two day seminar. The information is short, clear and concise providing, I hope, the clarity and advice that will benefit readers in a most practical way.

This book is not all encompassing — in fact, I have deliberately left out certain areas of the film industry from my discussion, such as film production. The reason for this is that I have read many good books on film production so why go there! My book covers the independent film business and specific topics that I view as important in providing the readers with practical and functional advice and tips, based on decades of living the film business, day in and day out, that will help you attain your dreams and aspirations in the independent film business.

****

CONTENTS OVERVIEW

Why the segment order as listed below? Simply, it addresses what I view to be the most pressing areas that filmmakers need to focus on and become most aware of in terms of the business aspects of the independent film industry.

SEGMENT ONE – Marketing & Distribution

Marketing and distribution, to most indie filmmakers, are the two most misunderstood topics in the whole filmmaking process. Most filmmakers concentrate on getting money to shoot their creation, their script. In many cases, little or no thought is given to who their target audience is or how they intend to sell and distribute their film once completed. This segment will address many areas that will help guide filmmakers in understanding the importance and relevance of marketing and distribution as part of the whole process.

CASE STUDY - "Serenity Farm" - from inception to screen, an ultra-low budget feature film

A discussion on the journey of making an ultra-low budget independent feature film -This film is still being produced at the time of publishing. It is a summary dialogue on how this film was put together and shot. A truly practical insight into producing a low budget feature film.

SEGMENT TWO - Selling

This segment deals with the idea that your film is indeed a product and requires a detailed knowledge of the avenues a filmmaker has available to them to assist in the process of selling/licensing their product. How much is a film worth? The answer is zero unless someone wants to buy it!!!! Think about that statement for a second!!! As filmmakers, there is a major knowledge gap in this area and this segment will help top up your knowledge quota and provide you avenues for potential film sales.

SEGMENT THREE – Film Financing

The nemesis of all independent filmmakers and film people in general. How do you acquire funding to shoot your film? For over 25 years I have used and exploited many ways to finance films, including financing my own films more than once. I have tried hundreds of ways, and lucky for me, many have worked. Some have failed miserably. My extensive practical experiences in film financing have helped me put together an extensive array of film financing strategies, some practical approaches, advice and tips to help you in this very frustrating and difficult arena.

SEGMENT FOUR - Creative & Producing

The creative process and producing a film usually includes extensive discussion on the production process. Here, I avoid that production area, other than in mentioning many good books that are available for filmmakers on the production process of filmmaking. I have focused on certain specific topics that I feel can benefit the filmmaker, director, writer, actor, etc. in the independent film world; which includes discussions on scripts, what is a producer, what do they do and some interesting Hollywood do's and don'ts.

****

WARNING!!
YOU WILL BE EXPOSED TO AN EXTREMELY
HIGH LEVEL OF VERY USEFUL
INFORMATION.

CONTENTS

SELLING 63

FILM FINANCING

CREATIVE/PRODUCING

****

MARKETING/DISTRIBUTION

HIGHLIGHTS OF THIS CHAPTER...

TRADITIONAL FILM MARKETING APPROACH

NON-TRADITIONAL FILM MARKETING APPROACH

FILM DISTRIBUTION

MEDIA RIGHTS — WHAT ARE THEY?

FOUR OPTIONS TO SELL YOUR
COMPLETED FILM

HYBRID DISTRIBUTION SOLUTION

NINE STEP PROGRAM FOR A SUCCESSFUL
FILM DISTRIBUTION STRATEGY

12 THINGS TO CONSIDER WHEN
SELECTING A DISTRIBUTOR

THE HITS & THE BOMBS!

MARKETING/DISTRIBUTION
"Do It Yourself?"

Independent Film Business 2010 - As theatrical release windows shrink, home video revenues dip, and high definition DVD struggles to meet expectations, filmmakers, filmed content distributors and media investors are searching to understand the online video world. Marketing and distribution have never before been in such a state of change and chaos, especially for the independent filmmakers! However, such a state can spawn amazing opportunities.

How to sell your completed independent feature film 2011
- **Option #1...Studios – forget it!**
- **Option #2...Mini Majors – don't bother**
- **Option #3...Traditional**
- **Option #4...Hybrid**

Continue reading for a full analysis of these options...

Every film, big or small, cultural or aiming directly at a mainstream audience, is trying to attract investors, public support, a director, a cast, distributors and, hopefully, a cinema going public. No matter how good a film is...without a well thought out and cost effective marketing campaign it has little chance of success in a very crowded and competitive market place. In today's dynamic entertainment environment movies are struggling to attract consumers and remain profitable. Challenges such as piracy, digital theft, competition, overlapping movie campaigns, media fragmentation, and audience saturation are forcing marketers to stretch their film budgets and make every dollar as effective as possible. Today's filmmakers confront a difficult reality; the game plan by which they've played for years is being challenged and there is a call for new, innovative ways to drive box office sales. In the historically used traditional model corporate marketers spend marketing dollars on messages aimed at a target audience. The marketing team creates a message, purchases media, and sees that the message is delivered. Given the fragmentation of media today ....PROBLEMS!!

MARKETING VS DISTRIBUTION – Understand the Difference

Marketing - In the motion picture industry, the marketing people devise, develop, and plan the publicity, promotion, and advertising of a movie. They create the media plan and execute the marketing strategy.

Distribution - The distribution of a film is the process through which a film is made available to an audience. This task may be accomplished in a variety of ways; for example, with a theatrical release, a DVD/home entertainment release or a TV broadcast and finally via the internet. A film distributor is a company or individual responsible for releasing films to the public either theatrically or for home viewing (DVD, VOD, Download, and TV etc.).

In many industries the distribution department may not be involved in the creation of the marketing plans and material...but, in the movie industry marketing and distribution often are one. The motion picture distributor is not only responsible for licensing movies to be shown in theaters (this is referred to as theatrical) and for contracting the rights for viewing on television, cable, DVD, video's etc. -they are also responsible for supervising the creation of the marketing strategy, the market research activities, the prints and advertising budget, the creation of the advertising, publicity and promotional material and the creation of the media plan. The motion picture distributor also supervises and controls the distribution of the marketing materials and the execution of the marketing plan at both the national level in the key markets and at the point of sale.

An independent film, or indie film, is a feature film that is produced mostly outside of a major film studio. Independent films are sometimes distinguishable by their content and style and the way in which the filmmakers' personal artistic vision is realized. Usually, but not always, independent films are made with considerably lower budgets than major studio films. Generally, the marketing of independent films is characterized by a potential limited theatrical release designed to build word-of-mouth or to reach small specialty audiences or just directly to DVD, TV or internet.

In today's world, one needs to clearly differentiate between the traditional approach to marketing and distribution and the non-traditional approach. What do I mean by this and how does it affect the independent film industry? The internet has materially changed the landscape of both marketing and distribution and if one can look into the future the internet will play an even more important role in these two important areas of the independent film industry.

In film marketing, the traditional marketing approach would include television (network/cable/syndication), newspapers/magazines, radio, outdoor billboards, trailers, product placement, publicity, EPK's, promotional tours, merchandising and in theatre promotion. The non-traditional would include online marketing capabilities and the new wave of technology such as smartphones. Both categories should work in harmony to maximize the marketing benefits and increase potential revenue for the film.

MARKETING

Independent filmmakers' first rule of marketing – start early and keep focused on your target audience and how to monetize those consumers. What is the point of making a movie and no one knowing about it? – Marketing is the key.

Marketing is a very important element in the world of film. In fact, studios are marketing machines and focus a great deal of time on marketing. Independent filmmakers should learn from the majors as they truly understand marketing. Although the world of internet and social networking has them a bit stumped, they will learn fast enough.

The majors ensure that the marketing personnel are involved in each film from project inception. "From cradle to grave" - was used at 20th Century Fox to state the involvement of marketing in the film process. After all, what is the point of making a film if no one wants to see it or should I say, pay to see it? What a novel concept that I often see totally ignored by many independent filmmakers. Why spend all that time and effort without doing research into the potential audience that will want to see your film? How big is that audience? How do you target that audience and how do you get your message to that audience in a cost efficient and effective way? These are fundamental marketing questions that rarely get asked upfront by independent filmmakers. It truly is... *"IT'S MARKETING STUPID!"*

Note to Producers: Ensure you think marketing at the time of inception of your film idea/your film synopsis/your film script...and then when you are trying to raise funding to make the film, your marketing strategy is an important part of your presentation to investors.

No matter how good a film is, without a well thought out and cost effective marketing campaign it will have little chance of success in a very crowded and competitive market place.

WHAT IS MARKETING?

Marketing is the process of building profitable customer relationships by creating value for customers and capturing value in return. It is the activity and processes for creating, communicating, delivering, and exchanging offerings that have value for movie goers...OR IS IT...the use of some form of media to make us purchase something we don't want, can't afford, at a price we don't like and with a product quality that is guaranteed to fall apart very soon... or in film language, to persuade us to see a film that stinks?

Today's filmmakers/marketers are empowered by more detailed consumer data, able to micro-target messages, interactively engage film goers with a whole new level of intimacy and frequency and customize to movie goers demands and wants.

Marketing is so simple...

The four steps to successful marketing and implementation include:

➢ Analyze your customers and the business environment in order to...
➢ Identify key opportunities to better and more profitably meet customer needs and...
➢ Figure out how to act on those opportunities, and then...
➢ Implement your plan...

A film should...

➢ Satisfy movie goers needs
➢ Build customer relationships
➢ Create value/get value

FIVE STEPS TO A SUCCESSFUL FILM MARKETING STRATEGY

1) *Understand the marketplace and the needs and wants of the customer.*

   Understand the type of film you wish to make (the product – genre/production cost/value etc. - the film package) and look at the customers wants, needs and demands to identify a potential market for your film.

2) *Design a customer driven marketing strategy.*

   What customers will we serve? We need to select customers that can be served profitably; therefore, we need to isolate and then target our audience. In addition, we need to position (budget/genre) our film to attract that audience and differentiate (this film is different) our film from other films that are similar in genre/type. How can we serve these customers best? By defining a value proposition...The set of benefits or values a filmmaker promises to deliver to consumers in order to satisfy their film going needs.

3) *Construct a marketing program that delivers superior value to customers.*

   Customers Perceived Value - The customers' evaluation of the positive difference of your film relative to those of a competing film.

   Customer Satisfaction - A film's perceived performance relative to customers' expectations. Marketing is all about managing the perceived value of your film.

4) *Build profitable relationships and create customer delight.*

   This is the overall process of building and maintaining profitable customer relationships by delivering superior customer value and satisfaction. It deals with all aspects of acquiring, keeping and growing customers.

5) *Get value back from customers.*

   They purchase the ability to view your product through whatever delivery channel they wish...and hopefully the word of mouth filters through the social strata and more people want to see the film.

THE SIX "MAGIC" FILM MARKETING PRINCIPLES

1) *Segmentation* – Select the audience demographics you wish your film to focus on.
2) *Targeting* – Target that group by offering your audience what they want.
3) *Positioning* – Place your film in a clear, distinct and desirable place (relative to competing films) in the minds of your target audience.
4) *Product Differentiation* – Make your film have a unique story/ approach/ quality that is different to other films of this type.
5) *Competitive Advantage* – Filmmakers need to gain an advantage over films in the marketplace by providing film goers greater value by unique story/ unique twists etc. to separate the film from all the clutter and other films out there.
6) *Value Proposition* – What the film has to offer and where it stands/ positions itself with all its attributes is the films value proposition. The film has to deliver those values otherwise film goers will not respond.

LET'S LOOK AT AN EXAMPLE
Thriller/horror film "Serenity Farm"

This film is actually being shot as this book is being written and the concept and story is my own creation. As I was developing the story I looked carefully into the six principles identified above.

1) *Segmentation* – I specifically identified an audience of young males, age 14-28.
2) *Targeting* – Young males aged 14-28 who like horror type films and enjoy the thrill ride and that is what my story would provide.
3) *Positioning* – My story would be clearly identifiable as a thriller/ horror and be of that genre.
4) *Product Differentiation* – Yes to the thriller/horror genre but the story had to provide uniqueness and a hook for the audience. This I did with the story being set in old concrete bunkers/tunnels with creatures that inhabited these tunnels and characters being trapped deep inside these scary tunnels.
5) *Competitive Advantage* – My film has to provide something different to the audience that will entice them to watch. The story, the location and the uniqueness of the tunnels would help provide

a competitive advantage compared to other thriller/horror genre films being released.

6) **Value Proposition** – The film has to deliver to the audience what it promises both in story, production value, locations and be true to the genre of the film.

THE SEVEN IMPORTANT RULES FOR FILM MARKETING
1) Know your genre
2) Know your target market / know your buyer
3) Know the size of your target market
4) Know how to get to your target market
5) Come up with an effective and cost effective marketing strategy
6) Know your competition
7) Start marketing from inception and keep doing it

In today's world, with the ever increasing importance of the internet/ social networking and buzz marketing, it is of paramount importance to ensure your online marketing begins as soon as possible as it takes time to build up a following/community.

AS A FILMMAKER... EVALUATE YOUR FILM
➢ *Commerciality* - evaluation of the film.
➢ *Budget* - negative cost – size of budget to potential return.
➢ *Cast Appeal* – any marketable actors.
➢ *Director Appeal* – marketability of director/ past films, etc.
➢ *Gender Appeal* – does the film have more appeal to either sex?
➢ *Revenue Markets* - both domestic and foreign potential - horror and family genres are usually popular all over the world - romantic comedies may be limited in certain foreign countries.
➢ *Timing* - is your film genre/type popular at this time?
➢ *Previous films* of actors/directors - past successes can help.
➢ *Genre* - certain genre can be better to market for - horror is good - drama may present more challenges.
➢ *Controversy* – can be beneficial but also can be negative.
➢ *Possible Awards* - film festival awards especially if well-known festivals are a major plus and of course award shows such as the Oscars/Golden Globes etc. can be significant revenue boosts.

> *Locations* - exotic or unusual locations of films can assist in marketing to attract audiences.
> *Effective Marketing Campaign* – the more marketing the better but it needs to be targeted.
> *Marketing Budget* – independent films usually have limited budget therefore effective marketing is a must.
> *Well Known From Another Property* - e.g. book/comic - can be beneficial if product is well known.
> *Target Audience/Positioning* – essential to know who your film is targeted to.
> *Marketability* - Understand what is attracting an audience to any given film - look to trailers, posters etc. - are they effective? - actors/director/genre.
> *Playability* - The way the film satisfies its audience - the level of satisfaction - word of mouth.

TRADITIONAL FILM MARKETING APPROACH

For decades the marketing gurus had certain tools at their disposal to create marketing campaigns with. These tools have virtually remained the same for many years until in the mid 1990's. Then the internet popped up and has subsequently changed the face of marketing forever. However, the traditional marketing approaches and the tools associated with it are still an integrated part of the marketing of film landscape. It is just that now new non-traditional marketing tools and approaches are available to enhance or totally confuse the marketing gurus of film marketing or both!

The object of film marketing is to build visibility and awareness, convincing the audience that this film is a must see, with desire peaking as it opens. The advertising and publicity campaign will reach the target audience as efficiently and frequently as practicable. A combination of word of mouth and further promotion will give the film "legs" during its release.

TRADITIONAL MARKETING CAMPAIGNS CONSIST OF THREE CATEGORIES

1) *Advertising* - Advertising is a form of communication that typically attempts to persuade potential customers to purchase or to

consume more of a particular brand of product or service. *Print *Television *Radio *Merchandising/Product Placement *Limited Internet

2) **Publicity** - Publicity is the deliberate attempt to manage the public's perception of a subject.
*Poster & Artwork *The Copy *Press Kit/EPK *Interviews *Trailers *Premiers/Screenings *Festivals

3) **Promotion** - Promotion involves disseminating information about a product.

- *Above-the-line promotion (ATL):* Promotion in the media. (e.g. TV, radio, newspapers, internet and cell phones)
- *Below-the-line promotion* (BTL): All other promotion. Much of this is intended to be subtle enough for the consumer to be unaware that promotion is taking place. (e.g. sponsorships, product placement, endorsements, sales promotion, merchandising, PR, personal selling, third party tie-ins, merchandising, festivals/ award shows)

TRADITIONAL MARKETING TOOLS IN MORE DETAIL

Let us look in more depth at the traditional marketing tools that the filmmaker has available. Of course, many of these tools depend on the size of your film's marketing budget – whether it is a major budget (studios can average $40m per film) or just limited marketing funds for a small low budget feature.

Television and Radio

- Paid advertising (30-second TV commercials) - placed broadcast and cable TV which are the main vehicles for advertising movies to audiences. TV is effective because it is an audio-visual medium – like film – and can deliver to a vast audience quickly. This is crucial because films typically are in cinemas for a short period.
- TV placement - full episodes of television talk shows like *Oprah*; entertainment news programs like *ET*; news programs with entertainment segments. Also included in this category would be interviews with actors and directors which are filmed en masse at a hotel with local and national entertainment reporters which are featured on local shows, cable networks and entertainment orientated programs.

- Behind-the-scenes documentary-style shows which are focused towards HBO and other mainstream paid channels.
- National, regional and local radio advertisements for films.
- Rental videos and DVD advertising with advance trailers, longer previews, or behind-the-scenes footage.

Print Media

- Paid advertisements in newspapers, magazines, etc.
- Comic special editions – merchandising.
- Paid co-advertising of a product with the film.
- Promotional giveaways – eg. food/toy combinations at fast food chains.

Film Promotional Tour

- Film actors, directors, and producers appear for television, radio, and print media interviews about their involvement in the production and making of the film. Interviews are conducted in person or remotely. During film production, these can take place on set. After film release, key actors/director makes appearances in major market cities personally, or participates remotely via "satellite" or telephone.

In Theaters/Cinema Lobbies

- Trailers are the bread and butter of the traditional marketing approach and they are focused and delivered directly to movie goers. They screen in theaters before movie showings. A 190 second burst of compelling, visual interpretation of the film's story to entice and interest the general public.
- Film Posters – artwork as a visual enticement to the general public of the film's story and appeal.
- Standups - freestanding paperboard life-size images of figures from the film.

Internet

- Creation of official film websites to provide in depth information about the film to interest the movie goer.
- Limited Buzz/Viral marketing through blogs/Facebook and film trailers and video user-generated-content.

Merchandising/Product Placement

- The licensing of film related imagery/characters can be both lucrative financially and great marketing for the film. Star Wars is a great example. Placing well known objects or products in a film can also provide revenue and in conjunction with the manufacturer provide co-operative advertising for the film.

Award Shows/Film Festivals

- Many films gain marketing exposure through award shows - e.g. Foreign Press Assoc., Oscar etc. and/or entry into major film festivals such as Cannes Film Festival.

Film Trailers

There are two main types of trailer:

- Teaser/Advanced Trailer
- Regular Trailer

Trailer considerations are: Target Audience, Positioning, Cast, Director, Genre, Special scenes from film, Story concept.

Teaser or Advanced Trailer - 90 seconds long - occurs before production starts

➤ *Creation*
  - Still Photography
  - Key Scene
  - Special Footage
  - Actual Footage
  - Graphics Only
  - Voice Over/Music

➤ *Process*
  - Big Idea
  - Script It
  - Storyboards

Regular Trailer - 2- 3 minutes long

➤ *Creation*
  - Well known stars? – actors/directors
  - Genre
  - Big budget effects
  - Story line; usual/intriguing – selling point
  - Film's title – communicate what film is about
  - Characters – sympathetic – help with audience
  - Sub-plots – can they help with wider audience
  - Magical place – transport audience
  - Subject – tap into audience fears
  - Locations – worldwide attractions

➤ *Process*
  - Use actual film footage
  - Ideas? - way to go based on the film
  - Multiple versions!

Artwork/Print Ads

Important to understand the direction of the marketing campaign in regards to positioning, genre and target audience. There are six elements Involved.

- ➤ Key Art
- ➤ Title Treatment
- ➤ Copy – Names, Awards, Reviews, Taglines, Actors/Director, etc.
- ➤ Billing - SAG Rules & Contract Stipulations
- ➤ Layout
- ➤ Taglines

Electronic Press Kits (EPK's)

A very important marketing tool - EPK's go to TV stations, Press, Cinemas, DVD stores. Contents of EPK's may include:

- ➤ Featurette (25 min. - behind the scenes/interviews)
- ➤ Trailer (teaser/regular)
- ➤ B-Roll Footage (informal footage during filming)
- ➤ Sound Bites (cast answering questions from interviewer - off camera)
- ➤ Short Newsy Stories
- ➤ TV Clips (TV coverage of film)
- ➤ Music Video/Sound Track
- ➤ Poster/Artwork
- ➤ Length – Varies up to and can exceed 30 minutes

Unit Publicist

Prepares publicity material and obtains press coverage before/during/ after/production.

- ➤ Synopsis of Film
- ➤ Bios of Cast/Director/Producer, etc.
- ➤ Good Production Stories
- ➤ Newsworthy Stories
- ➤ Press Visits
- ➤ Local Press
- ➤ Press Junkets
- ➤ Work with Unit Photographer – Photo Log/Video Clips
- ➤ Prepare Press Kit
- ➤ Website Copy & Internet Copy

Still Photographer

The photographer must understand the film marketing angle of the film. Photos must include:

- ➤ Lead Cast
- ➤ Supporting Cast
- ➤ Scene Shots
- ➤ Blue Screen Shots
- ➤ Background Set

- ➤ Locations
- ➤ Teen Mag Shots
- ➤ Director Shots
- ➤ Local Interest
- ➤ Action/Mood Shots

NON-TRADITIONAL FILM MARKETING APPROACH

If one assumes that the introduction into the traditional marketing mix of internet/online components such as a website can be included as part of the traditional model approach there are also certain elements that have developed over the last few years that can be called non-traditional. The non-traditional refers to components that have been created by technology in the 2000's and have largely been part of the internet explosion and the use of the internet as a marketing tool.

Today's new media marketing avenues:
- ➤ *Official Film Website*
- ➤ *Social Networking - Blogging/Twitter/Facebook/MySpace*
- ➤ *Online Film Communities*
- ➤ *Sponsorship/Social Marketing*
- ➤ *Tie–Ups with MySpace/Facebook/Moviefone/Fandango/Sharing/ Word Of Mouth*
- ➤ *UGMC – User Generated Media Content/YouTube*
- ➤ *Flash Display Ad – Basic Web Display and Banner Ad*
- ➤ *Rich Media Display*
- ➤ *More Advanced Web Display, Banner Ads with Interactivity, Video, Audio, Etc.*
- ➤ *Trailer Placement – many new platforms*
- ➤ *Viral Campaign – Buzz Activity*
- ➤ *E-Mail Blast – Mass E-Mailings*
- ➤ *Smartphone/Mobile/Cell Phones*
- ➤ *Play-Date Information and other info to help create buzz.*
- ➤ *On Line Virtual – Ads For Virtual Communities/Video Games*
- ➤ *Search Marketing - SEO*
- ➤ *Behavioral Marketing – Focus on movie goer communities*

It is important to fully grasp how marketing has changed in recent years especially relating to content and film/TV product.

- Technology has given consumers amazing access to whatever content they want and control over when they receive it — *anytime, anyplace, anywhere.*
- People want to be connected to other people who have similar interests, lifestyles and hobbies. Consumers are willing to give up significant information - new areas of content driven sites that will lead to new sources of revenue and new avenues to connect with consumers about film.

NON-TRADITIONAL MARKETING TOOLS IN MORE DETAIL

We have discussed some of the more important categories in the traditional marketing model now let us discuss some of the more important categories in the non-traditional model and ways to actively engage your online potential film audience.

Social Networking: Build your own social network for your film project utilizing Facebook Fan Page, Twitter or LinkedIn. Use YouTube as a video marketing tool that always links back to your film's website. Use forum marketing and guest posting on related blogs.

Certainly, marketing your project on Facebook is great and a filmmaker can have a major following on Facebook - but how do we turn these followers in to paying customers — i.e. wanting to see your film and pay for it either via online distribution or via DVD sales, etc. Converting fans or friends into paying customers is a very important aspect of social networking media. Be careful as Facebook is a social networking media not a buying medium. Social networking media is a great way to connect with people but it is only one of many marketing tools an independent filmmaker needs to market their film. Remember to seriously analyze the marketing section of this book and evaluate all the many tools for promotion that are available including official film websites, blogging, partnerships, URL links, etc.

Facebook Ads: Requires a budget and needs to be targeted.

Blogs: The use of blogs for film marketing has proven to be effective in helping stimulate word of mouth. Certainly it is also helpful in both blogging and with twitter that you are able to monitor activity concerning your film and the comments made about it. Technorati is a search engine that will assist you in tracing blogs etc. concerning your film title. Technorati is a blog search engine and directory. The site has become the definitive source for the top stories, opinions, photos and videos emerging across news, entertainment, technology, lifestyle, sports, politics and business. Blogging can be utilized for film marketing in a number of ways.

Twitter: Twitter is social networking/micro blogging to the general public; enabling its users to send and read other users' messages called *tweets*. These text based posts are up to 140 characters displayed on the user's profile page.

Social Plugins: Social plugins let you see what your friends have liked, commented on or shared on sites across the web.

UGMC - User Generated Media Content: Generally includes digital content produced by general public including digital video, podcasting, blogging, smartphone video/stills, and wikis. The advent of user-generated content marked a shift among media organizations from creating online content to providing facilities for amateurs to publish their own content.

Smartphones: The advances in the technology of cell phones and the improvement in delivery services (3G/4G) which enables personalized customer focus in delivering film information, schedules and video has created new avenues to market film materials.

Official Film Website: Your independent film must have its own official film website. This website is an important online part of your film's marketing strategy. This site should reflect all aspects of your film project and as a marketing tool it must present the values and benefits you wish to convey to your audience about your film. The film website should include as much of the following as possible and be constantly updated to remain fresh.

- *Bio's: Cast/Director/Main Crew/Music, Etc.*
- *Production Notes*
- *Production Footage*
- *Articles/Press Notes*
- *Artwork/Poster*
- *Featurette*
- *Film Trailers*
- *Sound Bites*
- *B-Roll*

- *Music Video*
- *Links To Other Sites*
- *Tie-Ins*
- *Merchandising*
- *Updates*
- *Competitions*
- *Distribution/Release Schedule*
- *Contact/Member Mailings Lists*

10 things a producer should know about an official film website.

1) Select a great name/URL
2) Use SEO keywords
3) Simple but interesting
4) Get a logo
5) Update your site with good content regularly
6) Build up contacts
7) Link with film communities and film sites
8) Generate interesting blogs about your film etc.
9) Connect your site with social networking – Facebook/YouTube/ Twitter/LinkedIn
10) Ensure you have video content

SEO - Search Engine Optimization: The process of improving the visibility of a website/ page in search engines. The higher on the search page and more frequently a site appears in the search results list, the more visitors it will receive.

Viral Buzz Marketing: Buzz marketing captures the attention of consumers and the media to the point that people talk about the film, because the message is perceived as entertaining, fascinating, and/or newsworthy - the word of mouth approach – an age old concept applied to 21st century technology! This concept is an important element of 21st century film marketing.

Buzz building plays a role within the context of a movie differentiation strategy, in that it helps to achieve a competitive advantage over other films in the market place. Buzz marketing plays a role in cutting through the clutter and capturing the attention of consumers and media.

What is buzz marketing, word of mouth, viral marketing and what does it means to independent film marketing?

➢ *Buzz Marketing:* The practice of gathering volunteers, either formally, by actively recruiting individuals who naturally set cultural trends, or informally by drawing "connectors"- people who have lots of contacts in different circles who can talk up their experiences with folks they meet in their daily lives.

➢ *Word Of Mouth:* Process by which one person informally influences the actions of others; key characteristic of this influence is that it is inter-personal and informal and takes place between two or more people who are independent.

➢ *Viral Marketing:* An internet-driven strategy that enables and encourages people to pass along a marketing message and engage in word of mouth – like a virus!

The Core of Buzz Marketing: If you are a filmmaker the world just described above is a very important one. It will help you possibly gain distribution and/or assist in generating potential revenue.

Buzz Marketing Implementation:

➢ What is special? - What is unique about your product that will interest people?

➢ Find a "buzz" hook - Need a hook to encourage people to talk about your product.

➢ How to start the buzz - Go to agencies that do this or go to "connectors" or do something newsworthy – get into tabloids or Perez Hilton!

➢ Include viral marketing - Draw people to your websites; encourage them to blog and social network about your product; use YouTube; be internet creative.

➢ Search for paths to spread the buzz - Use TV shows; tabloids; events; competitions, etc. to extend the spread.

➢ Calls for action - Create interactivity; surveys; competitions; location events.

➢ Create excitement!

Web Marketing Terms:

• *Conversion/Conversion rate:* Ability to get a visitor to your site/page to act and do something specific, usually click or buy the product. The rate of conversion is the % that click and act to those who just view.

- *Click/Click through rate:* Someone clicks on an advertisement or site and that click takes them to a sales page or home page of a product. The rate is defined as the average number of click through's per hundred ad impressions – as a %.
- *CPM/Cost per thousand impressions of your ad:* Impressions means a viewer sees your site/ad.

DIY FILM PROMOTION – 5 THINGS YOU SHOULD KNOW

As an independent filmmaker we can assume there is no huge marketing machine backing your newly completed film; therefore, the filmmaker must take charge of promoting his film. The following outlines some important items for DIY film promotion:

- ❖ *Have a Plan of Attack* - Each film is unique and requires a marketing and distribution approach all of its own. Therefore know your film; understand its audience and understand how you plan to attract that audience. A hybrid marketing and distribution plan is needed.
- ❖ *Marketing is from inception to screen, not just when it's completed* - Start your marketing early. Start at the time you conceptualize a film project and think about the audience and size of that audience and how you are going to attract that audience from inception of the story idea. This marketing concept must be enacted as soon as possible and be carried through the whole pre-prod-post process. The need is to engage the audience and get them involved in the film project. Remember marketing should include both traditional and non-traditional marketing tools. Ensure the film has a website, videos, trailers, stills, bios, sell sheet, EPK, etc.
- ❖ *Who is your audience?* - The major studios have wide demographics to target and the multi-million dollar advertising campaigns to capture those wide target markets. Independent filmmakers do not have that capability; therefore, being much more focused and specific on your target audience is a necessity. We can focus on a "niche" marketing approach that means a highly targeted group of people will be interested in your particular film and help to spread the word about your project. For instance, a low budget horror film with young teenagers as lead actors helps

clearly focus your marketing efforts on young people who would like this type of film. There are specific marketing approaches to help reach that demographic. Visit horror sites and horror social networking sites, blog, research those groups who express on Facebook, Twitter etc. their interest in horror films - plus go to horror magazines and their readership. Build a film website to appeal to that audience. Look at the marketing approach of Blair Witch – still a classic viral film campaign. Be original and inventive but always entertaining and interesting. Remember the more interesting your make your film and the more interesting content you put out into the film communities the better. Content is king!

❖ *Social Networking* - A major tool to assist an independent filmmaker in marketing their film. Rule of thumb is the 80/20 rule. While blogging, twittering or generally engaging your potential audience through social media, discuss only 20% about your project, while the other 80% is about information that will interest your audience. Similarly, engage with other bloggers and make comments – create a dialogue in the various social networking communities.

❖ *Into the Future* - The ability of independent producers to control their destiny in the marketing and distribution of their film comes at a price. That price is the amount of time, effort, research and know how required to generate potential revenue for the film in a marketplace that is constantly changing and developing. Certainly, the internet is the way of the future and as a platform of delivery it is most certainly a wave of the future. But, how can independents exploit this platform and gain a meaningful reward is yet to be fully revealed.

Film Marketing Changes 2010!

So many changes, so much new technology...

➢ *New Media:* Use of the internet/websites/SMS cell phone for both paid advertising and publicity - Viral marketing/social networking - Decline in print – mags./newspapers.

➢ *Box Office:* Big returns for blockbuster films but not so good for middle-range films in terms of box office – effects independent films.

- ➤ *Research:* General struggle to obtain accurate audience samples and data regarding the numerous emerging digital platforms.
- ➤ *Studios:* Was seven now six – loss of MGM - Time Warner/AOL deal ends.
- ➤ *Media Fragmentation:* Major expansion of media outlet channels - Internet, cable, satellite broad-band, wireless, mobile, MP3, iPod, and iPad.
- ➤ *Convergence:* Two types of convergence - both are driven by digitalization.
  - Device Convergence - the merging of the various delivery technologies by which content reaches the consumer - e.g. Smartphones
  - Content Convergence - the formatting and use of content, aided by the flexibility afforded by digitalization, to present the same content, information, stories, etc. on different platforms and in different ways.

DISTRIBUTION

WHAT IS DISTRIBUTION?

Most independent films never see the light of day and those that do make very little money, let alone fully repay the investors!

What is distribution? It is the final stage of the filmmaking process. To most filmmakers it is the stage that makes them the most uncomfortable and nervous. Without distribution the film will never get out to the general public and, therefore, will have very little potential to generate revenue.

Distribution entails knowledge of all the media rights involved in an intellectual property namely, a feature film. These rights encompass theatrical, DVD, TV and ancillary and more and more these days the online/internet rights. Remember, any contract concerning the rights of a film have to include the four elements of an intellectual property – namely, the geographical area (USA or Europe, etc. – It is common practice to call a country a "territory"); the rights involved (TV/DVD, etc.); the time period (five years?); and finally a dollar value ($$).

Distribution is all about getting the product, the film, to potential customers. For convenience the world is split into two large geographical areas namely domestic (USA & Canada) and foreign (the rest of the world). Just as a point of interest, the delivery system of broadcast (TV) is different in the USA/Canada compared to rest of the world. USA/Canada are NTSC format and the foreign market is PAL format. However, in 2009 a new standard replaced the NTSC, namely ATSC, which accommodates HD digital. For delivery of a film to TV stations etc. to occur to foreign territories the NTSC/ATSC still needs to be converted to PAL. With the advances of online delivery, "streaming" via the internet is a universal format that can play on any internet equipped computer.

In filmmaking we talk about "suspending your disbelief". Distributors want you to suspend your disbelief as they pull the wool over your eyes! The independent filmmaker finds the investors; takes all the risks; does all the work; takes months, even years to finish a film; has 100% control while making the film - BUT, then hands 100% control of the film to a stranger called a distributor and in time may or may not get some or all of the cost of the film back! Let's discuss the world of film distribution in relation to the independent filmmaker and provide insight and advice to help provide light in the distribution darkness.

MEDIA RIGHTS – WHAT ARE THEY?

As a filmmaker you need to understand which rights are available for which territories and how much you want to get ($'s) for those rights and for how long you wish to license them for. The following are the media rights concerned:

➢ *Theatrical* – cinemas
➢ *Home Entertainment* – DVD/Blue Ray
➢ *Pay Per View* - Broadcast viewing on pay TV which includes Video on Demand (VOD). View the film when you want.
➢ *Pay Television* – Broadcast on pay TV for paid subscribers, such as HBO and usually without commercials.
➢ *Satellite* – TV satellite markets within a territory and usually airs same time as Pay TV window.
➢ *Cable TV* – Broadcast for basic cable TV subscribers
➢ *Network/Free TV* – Broadcast on TV networks - CBS/NBC, etc.

➤ *Closed Circuit* - Hotels, airplanes, cruise ships
➤ *Other* - Military
➤ *Internet/Online* – Downloading or streaming
➤ *Ancillary* – Soundtrack, comic books, books, merchandising, spin-offs

These rights are governed by an order of distribution/time period - called a *"window"*. A window is a period of time during which the film is available for that specific media right.

It is important to understand these rights and the windows involved because if you are not clear on the best order of windows for the rights your film has available you could eliminate a specific media right due to losing its window. For instance, the VOD window can be eliminated (therefore revenue lost) if you decide to go directly to HBO Pay TV channel and not exploit the VOD window. It is not possible to go back to VOD once the film has been exploited on HBO. As a filmmaker it is important to be up to date with the rights available and what windows are exploitable. These windows change over time so pay attention! To ensure your film maximizes the exploitation of the rights and the window, make sure the license contract has a "holdback" included – the film cannot be shown on any other media for a specific time period.

A distributor is a company that takes on the responsibility of selling/ licensing a film to its various markets. This includes, but is not limited to theatrical, DVD, TV and ancillary markets both domestically and internationally. It is not unusual for the distributor to not only be responsible for licensing the films to the various media right markets but also for supervising the creation of the marketing campaigns and the marketing materials involved in the media plan at all levels of the marketing process – international, national, regional and local.

MEDIA RIGHTS – IN MORE DETAIL

Theatrical - Certainly, the theatrical option is traditionally the main launch option for studio films and also available to indie films but much more limited in scope. It is often not even a viable approach due to lack of marketing funds. However, theatrical is an important aspect of distribution and requires some discussion.

The traditional approach of studios is to have a wide release approach and blanket the country (wide release can be 3000+ prints).

This approach has an appropriate ad campaign of millions to match the country wide release. Such a major exposure of a film provides the platform for revenue in the following markets of DVD sales and TV revenue.

Three Main Theatrical Release Patterns:

1) Wide Release
   - 1000/4000 + Screens
   - Main studio vehicle
   - TV is expensive – national coverage, major $$$
   - Production/Negative cost of films very high

2) Limited Release
   - 50/700 + Screens
   - Target a specific demographic or studio wants to see how it goes

3) Exclusive or Platforming Release
   - More for specialty films that need to build word of mouth
   - Open wider slowly. A platform release option means releasing your film in one or two local theaters, start to generate significant buzz, and then slowly and strategically release it in additional theaters.
   - Example: NY/LA/Toronto – 2 theatres each city

Options for a limited theatrical release that are available for independent films are:

➢ Four Walling -

This option allows the filmmaker to book, market and promote a film in the markets they wish. They basically hire the theater and pay a fee, but the rest is the responsibility of the filmmaker. I have been involved in a number of these options. We four walled in three cities namely NY, LA and Chicago and hired a theater in each city.

➢ Service Deal -

Basically a filmmaker would hire a professional company that specializes in releasing films in theatres. Between them and the filmmaker a strategy is devised. It usually involves a limited release pattern that can be expanded to more cities if successful or curtail/amend if there are problems. Best examples of this strategy were "My Big Fat Greek Wedding" and the Mel Gibson "Passion of Christ" via Newmarket Films. Companies that can assist in the above approach are:

- Variance Films: www.variancefilms.com
- Emerging Pictures: www.emergingpictures.com
- Freestyle Releasing: www.freestylereleasing.com
- Balcony Releasing: www.balconyfilm.com
- Anywhere Road: www.anywhere-road.com

Non-Theatrical – Usually refers to the projecting of a film on a screen to an audience in a venue other than a cinema - e.g. College movie night.

Home Video/DVD - Home video is a blanket term used for pre-recorded media that is either sold or rented for home entertainment. DVD was adopted by movie and home entertainment distributors to replace the 1990's VHS tape as the primary means of distributing films to consumers in the home entertainment marketplace.

Residential VOD - Video on Demand (VOD) is a system which allows users to select and watch video content on demand. IPTV technology is often used to bring video on demand to television and computers. The residential statement refers to VOD direct to people's homes.

Pay Per View - PPV provides a service by which a television audience can purchase events to view via private telecast. The broadcaster shows the event at the same time to everyone ordering it (as opposed to VOD systems, which allow viewers to see recorded broadcasts at any time). Events often include movies, sporting events, and other special events such as professional wrestling, martial arts, and boxing.

Pay TV - Pay television, premium television, or premium channels refer to subscription-based television services, usually provided by broadcast, digital cable and satellite systems.

Network TV - A television network for distributing television content via a central operation that provide programming to many TV stations across the country. Networks in the USA include ABC, CBS, NBC and Fox.

Basic & Cable TV - Cable TV in the USA is a common form of television delivery, generally by subscription. Cable television programming is often divided between basic and premium programming. Premium cable refers to networks, such as HBO, Cinemax, Showtime, Starz, etc.

that scramble or encrypt their signals so that only those paying additional monthly fees to their cable TV system can legally view them (via the use of cable box or converter). This programming is commercial-free (except for promos in-between shows for the networks' own content). These networks command much higher fees from cable TV systems.

TV Syndication - Syndication is the sale of the right to broadcast television content to multiple individual stations, without going through a broadcast network. This is a well-developed TV content distribution system.

Foreign Revenue – more later...important topic.

NEW TECHNOLOGY/NEW TERMS/NEW PLAYERS

In today's world technology changes have introduced new terms, new revenue delivery platforms and new players to assist the independent filmmaker.

Downloading - To download means to receive data to a local system from a remote system. This would imply that the data is only usable when it has been received in its entirety.

Streaming - The term streaming indicates the receiving of data that is used near immediately as it is received, while the transmission is still in progress and which may not be stored long-term.

Netflix - offers both on-demand video streaming over the internet, and flat rate DVD and Blu-ray Disc rental-by-mail in the United States and Canada (streaming only). Netflix offers internet video streaming ("Watch Instantly") of selected titles to computers - currently the Watch Instantly service features more than 17,000 movies and recorded television shows. They have played a prominent role in independent film distribution. Netflix developed and maintains an extensive personalized video-recommendation system based on ratings and reviews by its customers, similar to the system used by Amazon.com. In May 2008 the first set-top-box to stream Netflix's Watch Instantly movies directly to televisions was released.

In 2010, Netflix reached an agreement with Warner Brothers Pictures to delay renting new releases for 28 days from their retail release in an attempt to help studios sell more physical media at retail outlets. A similar deal with Universal Studios and Twentieth Century

Fox was also reached. Netflix wishes to expand the video-streaming service to Apple's iPhone and iPod Touch mobile devices.

Redbox - is a competitor to Netflix. They use a kiosk approach. Rather than mailing DVDs - customers pick-up and return DVDs at self-service kiosks located in metropolitan areas. Coinstar, the owners of Redbox also plan to launch an online streaming service in early 2011.

YouTube - is the king of user generated video material from individuals – a video-sharing website on which users can upload, share, and view videos. YouTube displays a wide variety of user-generated video content, including movie clips, TV clips, and music videos, as well as amateur content such as video blogging and short original videos.

In November 2008, YouTube reached an agreement with MGM, Lions Gate Entertainment and CBS, allowing the companies to post full-length films and television episodes on the site, accompanied by advertisements in a section for US viewers called "Shows". This move was intended to create competition with websites such as Hulu. In January 2010, YouTube introduced an online film rentals service.

Video on Demand (**VOD**) - are systems which allow users to select and watch/listen to video or audio content on demand. IPTV technology is often used to bring video on demand to televisions and computers. Television VOD systems either stream content through a set top box, a computer or other device, allowing viewing in real time, or download it to a device such as a computer, DVR or portable media player for viewing any time. The majority of cable and satellite-based television providers offer both VOD streaming, including pay-per-view and free content, whereby a user buys or selects a film or TV program. It begins to play on the television set almost instantaneously, or downloads to a DVR rented from the provider, or downloads onto a computer for viewing in the future. Internet TV is an increasingly popular form of video on demand.

Platform Competition - Major satellite companies such as DirecTV are in competition with other delivery platforms to have you pay to see movies on their delivery format. The following highlights a comparison on a marketing approach used by DirecTV versus other competition:

	DIRECTV	NETFLIX	REDBOX
• New releases available same day as DVD (e.g. Inception)	YES	NO	NO
• New releases always in stock	YES	NO	NO
• Watch new releases in 1080p instantly	YES	NO	NO
• Late fees	NO	NO	YES
• Lost DVD fees	NO	Sometimes	YES
• 28 day wait to rent	NO	YES	YES

Mobile Media Devices – These include smartphones, iPods, gaming devices, iPads, etc. Media of many types can and are being downloaded to mobile devices - downloaded onto the device by podcasting or can be streamed over the internet. Digital applications include gaming, video, audio, downloadable ring tones and mobizines. A number of mobile operators are also investigating the viability of mobile TV.

MEDIA RIGHTS – REVENUE CYCLE/WINDOWS

The following clearly outlines the traditional revenue cycle of media rights that identify the window of revenue sources, that has until recently been viewed as the traditional model used as a standard in the film industry especially by the studios and to a lesser extent independent films.

Media Right	Beginning	Window
THEATRICAL	Initial theatrical release	6 months
NON-THEATRICAL (Airlines/Hotel)	3 months after initial theatrical release	12 months
HOME VIDEO/DVD	3-6 months after initial theatrical release	10 years
RESIDENTIAL VOD	6 months after initial theatrical release	
PAY PER VIEW	8 months after initial theatrical release	2 months
PAY TELEVISION	12 months after initial theatrical release	18 months
NETWORK TV	30 months after initial theatrical release	30 months
PAY TV – 2nd window	60 months after initial theatrical release	12 months
BASIC CABLE	72 months after initial theatrical release	60 months
TV SYNDICATION	132 months after initial theatrical release	60 months

These windows have changed over the years – both in order and time period. In recent years there have been major movements that have affected the traditional schedule of windows/rights order.

These changes include significant changes in the reduction of the time period assigned to relevant windows. The time between theatrical release and the DVD window has and continues to have that window reduced and in some cases the time period is very tight from release to DVD street time. Secondly, the internet (Amazon/Official film websites) has created a new window availability that requires attention. Thirdly, the advent of Redbox kiosks and their requirement for window adjustments to suit their business model needs addressing. The expansion of ITunes and the ability of VOD to provide instant download/streaming have an effect on windows/media rights order/timing.

COLLAPSING WINDOWS 2010

As stated, the whole traditional order and timing of windows (rights) has been in a state of change. A recent review of windows indicates the following trend:

➢ *VOD* – Includes internet, IPTV, digital cable and satellite VOD. Can start around one month after film ends its theatrical run. Have premium VOD on IPTV.

➢ *DVD* – Released two or three months after theatrical run.

➢ *VOD - second time round* – Begins 30 – 60 days after video release and prices are reduced.

➢ *Broadcast* – On terrestrial and cable channels about one year after theatrical run.

Windows will be changing and adapting as new technology comes available and matures in the market place. Keep your eyes on this as it affects your distribution and potential revenue dollars for the sale of your film. Make sure you understand the windows and ensure you maximize each right and the time available for exploitation.

STRATEGIES TO DISTRIBUTE YOUR COMPLETED INDEPENDENT FEATURE FILM

This book is truly aimed at the low budget independent feature film world - not the studios, not the mini majors and usually not the theatrical world, as the vast majority of low budget independent films never get theatrically released and as previously stated, most indie films never see the light of day. Remember the budget level we are discussing – low budget independent feature films.

Your film is completed now what? Here are some of your options to get the film distributed.

➢ **Option #1**: Go directly to a major studio – forget it!!
➢ **Option #2**: Go directly to a mini major – hardly!
➢ **Option #3**: Go directly for traditional approach - namely, sales agents/festivals/TV channels or DVD companies. This is still a viable option but needs to be evaluated for your needs. The traditional avenue for trying to sell your independent film was indeed to go to a sales agent. In my section entitled "Selling", I discuss at some length the topic of sales agents. There are many different forms of sales agents and here are a few of the those:

- Sales agent that sells all rights to all territories - including domestic.
- Sales agent that sells all rights to foreign only.
- Sales agent that sells all rights only to domestic.
- Sales agent that sells only TV rights for domestic.

Certainly, for the films I had the rights for, I would contact a sales agent that specialized with TV sales in the USA and allow him to make the sale to HBO, Starz, Showtime or Hallmark or Sci-fi channel. Their relationship with these TV channels and quantity of films they have supplied them over time provided them access that I could not have with the one or two films I represented. The sales agent would get the commission, but I would get a sale. Many of these TV channels need product so as a filmmaker do not ignore domestic TV channels as a potentially good revenue source.

To assist you in identifying which is which and who owns what, I provide you the following breakdown of the major pay TV players in the USA:

- HBO/Cinemax: 41m Subscribers
- Showtime/TMC/Flix: 61m Subscribers
- Starz/Encore: 47m Subscribers

(Buys some 250 independent films per year)

Note: DVDs by mail player Netflix could become a significant buyer for not only studio product but also independent films through the internet streaming service it offers to its 15m subscribers. If Netflix is successful in this area then ITunes and/or

Hulu might venture into competition for traditional pay TV rights/ windows that have been controlled by HBO, Showtime, etc.

➤ **Option #4:** HYBRID/ DO IT YOURSELF DISTRIBUTION (DIY) - Truly the future of independent filmmaking. But understand this approach is changing and developing as we speak. That being so - the avenues for revenue are also changing and developing. As yet they have a long way to go in replacing traditional DVD sales or TV sales. But, that will change in time – when, is a good question? Certainly, in the past filmmakers would only address the option of DIY as a last resort, but in today's market the DIY option has a number of viable financial avenues.

It would appear reasonable for filmmakers to look carefully at all options and based on today's market place, a hybrid distribution model would suit many filmmakers that want to license their film. The hybrid can encompass DIY online distribution options plus utilize the more traditional avenues of sales agents and TV sales, plus even a limited theatrical release.

HYBRID DISTRIBUTION SOLUTION – THE BEST COURSE OF ACTION

A low budget independent feature filmmaker should seriously contemplate the following option in order to try and maximize all the available avenues that can help generate revenue for his low budget film. These are the distribution avenues (any or all or just select which fits) that should be considered - but make sure all the areas discussed above regarding marketing your film are applied and executed to ensure maximum exposure of the film as these distribution avenues are exploited.

9 STEP PROGRAM... FOR A SUCCESSFUL FILM DISTRIBUTION STRATEGY

The following are variables that may or may not impact the filmmaker when deciding what the optimal distribution strategy for the film should be:

➤ Size of budget of the film
➤ The amount of time available
➤ The pressure to perform/sell

➢ Availability and amount of funds
➢ Knowledge of the distribution business
➢ Knowledge of marketing
➢ Legal/contract expertise
➢ Trust
➢ Reasonableness test

All of the above and I suspect many more, are factors that come into play when a filmmaker has to make decisions about the distribution options that are open. Once again, I must emphasize the importance of understanding who your film is aimed at and who will ultimately pay to see your film. As a filmmaker, answer these questions before you move forward with your film project.

➢ Who is the target audience for your film?
➢ What is the size of that target audience?
➢ How do you intend to reach that audience?
➢ What is the marketing strategy you are to employ?
➢ What distribution/rights offer you the best revenue potential?

In my many years of being in the independent film business, I have had to deal with many of the factors listed above on many occasions with many different types of films and at the finally analysis the filmmaker has to make choices based on the circumstances provided to him. Certainly, the ability to have funds to assist in marketing or to provide a limited theatrical release is a great benefit. Having personal contacts with a sales agent of a TV channel is also a great benefit. Understanding your target audience and how to market your film to them is another great benefit. Usually a filmmaker is faced with having to make judgment calls based on circumstances and those choices might not be optimal, but are the best option under the circumstances. Often there is pressure on a filmmaker to return the investment made during production. This pressure can cause the filmmaker to make choices that are not the best for the long term revenue potential of the film – the old "one in the hand is worth two in the bush" saying, can work both ways for a filmmaker.

Be reasonable and have expectations of your film's potential based on realism not fantasy. Not every indie film made for $14k can make over $100m!!! Based on that statement it is necessary to be reasonable. I remember a filmmaker I was representing at the AFM, turned down a good offer I presented to him from a major German company, as he thought the offer was too low and he had unrealistic expectations of a much bigger offer that will come along later at the AFM. Well guess what, no larger offer came along and the German buyer retracted his offer later that day as he found another film to buy. The film remained unsold to Germany through that AFM and, of course, when Cannes came along the film was no longer new and the buyers saw an opportunity to low ball as they thought the filmmaker might need to sell. Guess what! – He did need to sell and he instructed me to sell at 50% what was offered to me at the AFM.

STEP #1: Revenue Potential of the Film

Make a reasonable assessment of the revenue potential of the completed film (low, medium and high) based on your own research for the genre, type of film, production value and budget size. This film appraisal should show a potential of enough revenue to repay your investors. If not you are in really trouble!! Remember what I have said before – don't make a film and have investors, unless you know who your target audience is and what is reasonable to expect to sell the film for. If the amount you come up with before the film is made is less than the investors put in don't make the film - otherwise you will have some very unhappy people on your back! What a reasonable common sense statement that is - but let me tell you that such a statement often eludes a filmmaker!

Once the film is completed a filmmaker should get professional film people, agent's reps, etc. to provide sales estimates. The filmmaker can compile *low, medium and high revenue projections* from the potential sale of all the rights both domestic and foreign. Based on these projections the filmmaker can make future decisions of reasonableness as offers or sales begin to come to the filmmaker as the distribution avenues open up.

Step #1 allows the filmmaker to make decisions on distribution channels available that are feasible and reasonable for the film with the understanding that major studios and mini majors are not interested in your film.

STEP #2: Evaluate Distribution Options

The filmmaker must now fully evaluate all the options available for distribution. That means fully understanding all the various forms of rights and territories the film implicitly has as an intellectual property, namely domestic and foreign, theatrical, TV, DVD, internet, etc. How does one effectively make decisions on how to exploit each of these options? A number of the variables will come into play such as how much funds are available for marketing; how much time   the filmmaker has to exploit any one of these distribution options; how much knowledge and expertise has the filmmaker got in these areas. Many of these variables will dictate courses of action.

Do not forget film festivals as a means of marketing your film and to attract potential buyers/distributors.

STEP #3: Limited Theatrical Release – USA

Once again the filmmaker must make the evaluation as to the reasonableness and feasibility of a limited or platform release of a low budget indie film. The filmmaker must ask the question as to the money spent on a release compared to the financial benefit received for such a release. It is normal to expect to lose money from such a release, in terms of renting the cinemas and the cost of the advertising etc. compared to ticket sales. However, will the release benefit the film in other ways such as increased DVD, VOD or TV sales? Will the exposure of a theatrical release benefit the film in increased sales of other rights? This is a very difficult question to answer and for the filmmaker to evaluate. I have been involved in these decisions before and in those cases the decision to do a limited theatrical release was not a good one. Money was spent and the increased sales of the DVD and TV did not increase enough to counter the cost of the release. However, the theatrical release made the filmmaker and investor very happy, as it provided them with exposure and kudos that help them in their own career and personal achievement status.   Once again variables come in to play.   Will a theatrical release attract the attention of a major DVD distributor or a TV channel?

STEP #4: Domestic DVD distributor

We are assuming that no domestic or worldwide distribution company has picked up your film for worldwide exclusive distribution. Such companies as LionsGate or Summit (companies that can and do pick up titles for worldwide distribution but on a very limited basis) have passed on worldwide rights distribution of the film; therefore, as a filmmaker you look to the other options available.

Looking for a domestic DVD distributor should be explored before a DIY option comes in to play. There are a number of DVD distributors that can and do pick up low budget titles. The DVD market has certainly diminished over the last decade but can still be a lucrative source to receive an upfront payment and royalty deal and, of course, have the benefit of extensive distribution channels across the USA. An interesting option for a certain type of film is Wal-Mart.

Another option - Should going directly to these large DVD distribution companies in the US not be an effective avenue, an option could be to approach a domestic sales agent who has positive contacts with these DVD companies and they may be able to do a deal with them due to their relationship.

Internet - It is also understood that a filmmaker in today's online/ internet world has distribution outlets provided by the internet. This will include the sale of DVDs via the official film website and by using the social networking medium to generate buzz and hopefully sales of the film via DVD on the internet.

STEP #5: Domestic TV sale

Certainly a domestic TV sale can be very lucrative for an independent filmmaker. Once again the filmmaker must assess which TV channels are a suitable target based on the type of film, its genre, actors, etc. Certainly to approach major cable channels such as Hallmark or Sci-Fi channel etc. with the appropriate type of film can and has been effective - plus going directly to pay TV channels such as HBO or Starz is worth trying. In general, to go to networks is not an effective avenue as they tend to look to major releases. Going to cable/satellite channels for basic or premium satellite channels is available to all filmmakers but how successful is another question.

Another option - Should going directly to these TV channel companies in the US not be an effective avenue, an option could be to approach a domestic sales agent who has positive contacts with these TV channels (basic and pay). They may be able to do a deal with them due to the relationship of selling product to them over a long period.

With both domestic DVD and domestic TV, I have acted as a sales agent for films and also for my own films. I have approached these large media companies to obtain a distribution deal and have been successful in the past.

STEP #6: Domestic VOD

The VOD option for an independent is a relatively new avenue. It is true that the major TV companies such as HBO etc. have a VOD element to their viewing portfolio, but this is only accessed if a film is licensed by a major TV channel. This discussion is about the option if the film has not been licensed by a TV channel. There are still VOD options available to an independent filmmaker that are becoming an important part of the distribution matrix that can help provide additional revenue not previously available to indies. VOD outlets such as Amazon and iTunes can be accessed by indies; however, these outlets are already being protected in that it is now common for filmmakers to go through aggregators (e.g. Indie Rights) which then pass on the films to the VOD companies. This will be a growing area for revenue accumulation for indie filmmakers in the future. Please note – In this avenue marketing of your title is of paramount importance. It is the responsibility of the filmmaker to get their title known and to get people to download or stream it and generate the revenue. Amazon makes the title available, but who pays to see it is very much up to the marketing efforts of the filmmaker. The filmmaker has to have the time and some $ resources to generate an effective marketing campaign for the film -otherwise it will just become another title in a large database of films in the Amazon archives. Netflix is another major online distributor with over 100,000 titles on DVD and more than 12,000 choices to watch instantly. Netflix has focused on independent films who have submitted films to Netflix for distribution.

STEP #7: DTC DVD

The Direct to Consumer DVD distribution option (DTC DVD) is also an avenue that has recently matured and continues to mature and is available to indie filmmakers. Once again Amazon is providing an important distribution outlet - Amazon's Create Space (www.CreateSpace.com). This On-Demand service provides a full service order, manufacturing and delivery system as well as access to the millions of customers who use Amazon.

Note – Exploitation of media rights and their associated "windows" is an important element all independent filmmakers need to know as they evaluate the distribution avenues.

As stated, there is now a bevy of online services to assist filmmakers in DIY distribution. Examples of such companies include IndieFlix, Jaman and Babelgum (others include: Atom, Blip.TV, Film Annex, Snagfilms). They provide a platform for DIY – to build audience, self-distribute and produce revenue from their content and utilize ads to help generate revenue.

Details of **IndieFlix** are:

> ➤ IndieFlix is completely non-exclusive. Filmmakers are free to explore other outlets on their own.
> ➤ IndieFlix is never paid unless the filmmaker is paid. For all revenue, filmmakers receive 70% of net and IndieFlix gets 30% of net. "Net" means after costs.
> ➤ Filmmakers aren't locked in with IndieFlix. IndieFlix has four main revenue sources available but filmmakers are free to opt out of any of them.
> ➤ IndieFlix is a "filmmaker first" marketplace and distribution company. It is built to empower filmmakers to be both artist and entrepreneur and to make film festival screened work from all over the world available to the broadest online audience.
> ➤ IndieFlix exists to help independent filmmakers benefit as technology moves the internet and television closer together. As such, films sold at IndieFlix.com are not only available for DVD sales but also streaming online pay-per-view.
> ➤ Further, IndieFlix has created alliances with key online delivery platforms such as Joost, Hulu, Snag Amazon VOD, Netflix, iTunes and others. Some titles are on these outlets offering filmmakers more revenue opportunities at the same 70/30 split.
> ➤ A list of revenue sources currently available through IndieFlix along with any associated costs that must be paid out prior to calculating royalties:

- DVD Sales (duplication on demand and order fulfillment) $4.75 per unit is paid to DVD fulfillment company pool.
- Streaming 30-Day Rental (watch films on website while on internet) $1 per unit is paid to VOD delivery company pool.
- Subscription - Pay is based on the number of members.
- Distribution to third-party outlets -Revenue and costs vary for each outlet.

Certain key elements should be considered before venturing into utilizing such online distribution entities.

Firstly, *payment.* Many of the ad-based distribution sites encourage filmmakers to develop buzz marketing which generates more clicks, therefore more plays, which generates more advertising exposure and therefore more money. Some sites are strictly ad-based others include revenue from sales of DVDs, downloads, streaming, etc. At Film Baby, filmmakers set the price of the DVD and retain all proceeds, minus a $4 fee per DVD sold. At HungryFlix, filmmakers are offered a 60/40 split. At Jaman, revenue is generated through film rentals, purchases and ad-infused content.

Secondly, there is *promotion.* The more viewers of content - the more money is generated. Alliances are key to this venture for such sites. There are thousands of indie films so promotion is a vital element to ensure a filmmaker makes money. The promotion avenues are many and varied. Such avenues will include social networking and the free video sites on Facebook, Vodpod and Dailymotion, but this is relatively small compared to the major sites of iTunes and Netflix. Netflix, for instance, has over $200m to spend on marketing their products (usually traditional marketing tools plus online are used) every year - but word of mouth remains a powerful tool for marketing a film. Similarly, YouTube, via its "Screening Room" provides significant marketing for a film. In addition, if YouTube has overlay ads in the film, that ad revenue is also shared with the filmmaker along with sales from the DVD sales and iTunes downloads. Of course, obtaining a deal with one of these major online outlets is more difficult than the smaller sites – which do handle the promotion for a film. IndieFlix states that they will utilize social networking and other media sites, plus its alliances and partners, such as Joost, Amazon Video on Demand, Netflix, Hulu, etc.

to help promotion. Such sites help a filmmaker promote their film. These smaller sites provide a filmmaker an already established team of tech savvy business development and ad sales executives to assist in selling the film.

Finally, we have *protection,* namely copyright. The content submission agreement needs to be examined closely. The majority of online distributors are non-exclusive, with the filmmakers retaining all rights.

Can a filmmaker make money from these online distributors? The answer is yes. The question is more, how much. This depends on the type of content you are providing, the business revenue model being used and the advertising strategy and budget included. Certainly, the filmmaker can improve the sales of the film by being active in the marketing of their own film (using traditional and non-traditional approaches/tools) and increasing the viewership of the film on the distribution site showing the film. The idea of this new and developing online distribution platform is to have independent film producers sell their content on their own terms and control their own destinies.

DTC DVD distribution dictates the end user receives a physical DVD disc of the movie. Direct-to-Consumer (DTC) DVD distribution is an option that is easily accessible to independent filmmakers. However, marketing is so vitally important and is hard work for the filmmaker. Your options on delivery to consumers for professional quality DVDs is by either outsourcing the manufacturing of the DVDs and fulfilling the orders yourself (or also outsourcing the fulfillment function), or by utilizing an on-demand replication service like Amazon's Create Space (www.CreateSpace.com) who then takes the orders and does all the delivery for you. They will take a fee for those services.

The on-demand DVD distribution option appears to be a good alternative for independent filmmakers in that it is an affordable and low-risk way to make the film available without incurring startup costs and holding inventory. (The costs can be $2 - $5 per disc including DVD authoring, encoding, menus, cover art, packaging and fulfillment, depending on how many units per run. The bigger the unit order the cheaper it is.) The on-demand service provides you a full service order/ manufacturing/delivery system.

As a filmmaker, there is a need to market, market, market your product to consumers. Now you have to have a solid base to direct consumers to. You need know they will be fully serviced and you will get your accounting/royalty every month. Also, let's not forget that these distribution deals are non-exclusive so other distribution options are still available to filmmakers including traditional distribution options we have already discussed. One major marketing advantage with going with Amazon Create Space (www.CreateSpace.com), the biggest player in on-demand DVD distribution, is that you are guaranteed exposure to the tens of millions of customers who visit Amazom.com on a daily basis.

Note of Caution! - Releasing your film straight to DVD can create difficulty with the exploitation of other media rights. For instance, the release of the DVD will create a problem for a limited theatrical release option as a theatrical distributor would require a "window" before DVD release. That would be compromised by your own DVD distribution activities. Distribution "windows" need to be fully understood by the independent filmmaker as they have serious revenue issues.

Why Amazon "Create Space" for your DVD sales?

➢ No membership or DVD setup fees.
➢ Let your fans pick the format - easily sell your video content as DVDs and as video downloads.
➢ Free UPC assignment.
➢ A non-exclusive agreement keeps your distribution options open.
➢ They produce DVDs when customers order, so you never have to predict demand or hassle with order fulfillment.
➢ DVDs are eligible for listing on IMDb.
➢ Duplication and replication services are available.
➢ Multi-disc sets, multi-case collections, and combined DVD and CD sets are available.
➢ Sell your DVD, CD, MP3, or video download on Amazon.com and other marketplaces. Earn royalties on every sale that you

make without having to worry about inventory, minimum orders or setup fees.

Online Distribution leaders:

> Amazon: Online retailer who delivers content to TV, Computer, iPod and you can own or rent.
> Netflix: Internet video rental delivers to computer (watch now) or direct to TV (Roku box).
> Apple: Online enabled downloads to iPod, computer, TV - to own or rent.
> Google, YouTube: Online video streaming to mobile devices and computer for free streaming.

STEP #8: Digital Do-It-Yourself Distribution

Technology has provided the filmmaker with some interesting options for potential revenue that as time moves on could become significant. At the present time these revenue options are limited for the independent filmmaker; however, they must be examined for their contribution to independent filmmakers' revenue streams.

VOD (Video on Demand Distribution) - delivers the film to the end-user by download or by streaming to a device such as a computer or TV, etc. and is usually done instantaneously. A film can be watched anytime, anywhere, on any media device.

The basic method of delivery is quiet simple. The filmmaker signs a deal with a digital distributor and provides the distributor with a digital master, per specifications. Once delivered the distributor creates the movie files for the film to be uploaded to the distributor's servers. Once the film is fully uploaded it is available for customers to pay a fee to download your film and watch it. There are a number of such distributors who specialize in this delivery method. The VOD delivery method is instant, unlike the DVD delivery method that has become a traditional delivery method of a physical disc.

It is usual that the VOD distributors' licensing deals are on a non-exclusive basis, therefore, allowing the filmmaker latitude in various forms of delivery and with various types of distributors. From a revenue perspective VOD companies will prepare monthly accountings and, hopefully, send monthly checks based on customers' purchases of your film. Should a VOD distributor charge $9.99 for a download of a film to a consumer, a 30%-60% royalty can be expected to the filmmaker.

A few VOD distributors in today's marketplace are included below - but there are many and filmmakers need to do their own research prior to selection:

- Amazon Unbox: www.amazon.com/video-on-demand
- Apple iTunes: www.itunes.com
- Cinemanow: www.cinemanow.com
- Hulu: www.hulu.com

"Hulu" is a website that offers ad-supported streaming video of TV shows and movies from NBC, Fox, ABC, and many other networks and studios. Hulu distributes video both on its own website and syndicates its hosting to other sites. They also allow users to embed Hulu clips on their websites. In addition to NBC, ABC and FOX programs and movies, Hulu carries shows from other networks such as Current TV, PBS, USA Network, Bravo, Fuel TV, FX, NFL Sports, Speed, Big Ten Network, Syfy, Style, Sundance, E!, G4, Versus, A&E, Oxygen and online comedy sources such as Onion News Network. Hulu provides video in flash video format, including many films and shows. "Hulu Plus," a monthly subscription service, was launched on June 29, 2010.

Like the free version of Hulu, the video available on Hulu Plus also contains commercials. However, it offers subscribers an expanded content library in the form of full seasons and more episodes of shows already available through Hulu. Consumers can now also watch Hulu on their TVs by simply connecting a computer
with a streaming capable video card to the TV via HDMI or other connections.

Additionally, the Hulu Plus service, fully launched in November 2010, allows first-party access to Hulu from a variety of Blu-Ray linked TVs, iOS devices, gaming consoles, and set-top boxes.

In late June 2010, it was announced that a version of Hulu would be available to the iTunes App Store for the iPad, iPhone and iPod Touch running iOS4 or higher. Viewing the content on Hulu, however, requires a subscription. On November 2010, Orb

Networks announced the Orb TV box which streams Hulu on the TV for free.

Hulu Plus, the monthly subscription package, unlocks the iPhone and iPod application that allows streaming all Hulu content from Wi-Fi and wireless data networks via a dedicated app that users may download freely.

Aggregators – It appears that the VOD distributors like to use the services of VOD aggregators who are like VOD sales agents. Aggregators collect a number of the film titles and prepare them for submission in a particular manner to the VOD distributors – a middleman. This is now well established, so here are some of the aggregators that will assist you in getting your film to the VOD distributors:

- New Video (USA): www.newvideo.com
- Indie Rights (USA): www.indierights.com
- Cinetic Filmbuff (USA): www.cineticfilmbuf.com
- Content Republic (UK): www.contentrepublic.com

Marketing – It is important for the filmmaker to clearly understand how important marketing is in the online world. It's important to get your film on the list of films being offered by the VOD distributor, but it is also important to ensure that the consumer knows about the film. What use is it for a film to be on a list of hundreds of films offered by a distributor if the viewing public knows little or nothing about the film? MARKETING – either you or the distributor or both have to focus on marketing your film. All the marketing discussed above needs to be effective to get consumers to access your film. A buzz - a clear effective marketing effort.

VOD is still developing not only in the USA but all over the world. There is no doubt that the sale of physical DVDs will ultimately disappear and new technology delivery methods will totally replace this traditional method. That includes the online distribution set-ups we are discussing. VOD could become, in time, a major revenue source for the independent filmmaker, but, at present VOD revenue is limited.

Internet Distribution/Online Distribution -
"Where digital production has democratized filmmaking opportunities, the internet has democratized distribution and exhibition opportunities."
"The internet levels the playing field with its extremely low barrier to entry and unlimited distribution"
- Jacques Thelemaque, Pres. of Filmmaker's Alliance.
One of the only forms of media an independent filmmaker can compete on the same level as a studio!   The internet provides numerous benefits:

> Easy access to film information of all kinds (www.imdb.com)
> Convenient method to purchase film DVDs
  - Sell direct to public
  - Use known retailers Amazon/Createspace.com – usually known films
  - Drop shipping – Doba, Baker and Taylor
  - Renting – Netflix, Blockbuster, Redbox
  - Short Films - Atom Films and advertising – selling ad space
  - Blip.tv – syndicate films across number of sites
> Alternative film distribution channel (porn, horror, mainstream)
> As technical limitations of bandwidth, connection speeds, plus IP matters are improved full length films will become generally available
> Internet is global
> Window/ Internet release time
  - Traditional – Theatres, video, DVD, PPV, premium cable, network TV, basic TV and studios are vertically and horizontally integrated
  - Theatrical release is a platform for public awareness

Internet Film Distribution - Order of Events for a Filmmaker
1) Film website creation – ASAP
2) Facebook, Twitter & Blog – be active.
3) Constantly update with new content – pre/prod/post.
4) This all takes time – word of mouth
5) Blair Witch mode - sneak trailers, things of interest
6) Gather e-mail addresses

7) SEO + Submit your site's URL to search engines. (Keyword Tool -Google)
8) Film complete – start pitching webmasters for free banner space -one filmmaker to another
9) Begin exchanging links with other websites
   - attracts traffic
   - a site worth viewing
   - help you in search engines
10) Traffic monitoring software webtrends – analyze your traffic
11) Use site for update events – festivals/ local film communities
12) PR – use PR log for press releases

Internet Distributors -
Cinema Now / Atom Films / Cinema Pop / Entertaindom / Eveo / Hypnotic / Ifilm / LikeTV / Movie Flix / New Venues /Sputnik 7
You are only limited by your own imagination when dealing with the internet your website/social network!

STEP #9: Foreign! ...TV/DVD Plus
For the vast majority of independent films that get licensed in the global marketplace, foreign sales provide anywhere from 60% to 80% of the total revenue generated by the licensing of the rights of that film. Therefore, a filmmaker should pay a great deal of attention to foreign and how to maximize those foreign revenues. The sad truth is that for many US filmmakers the foreign marketplace is truly a mystery to them and their ability to understand how to exploit it even more so. At AFM 2010, much of the talk I heard from US independent filmmakers was all about DTC DVD and VOD – generally all focused on the USA scene. Yet from recent revenue figures these relatively new avenues of distribution count for a small amount of total revenue. Granted, over time that will change and DVD will fade out just like VHS. Delivery by internet will become the predominant indie film distribution system for films.

Foreign is still an important revenue source for independent filmmakers. DVD rights are still important though shrinking. Television rights are still important and can generate significant revenue for indie films. As the VOD market expands across the world, this area will become more significant also.

Internet rights - As a note, many independent filmmakers who understand the foreign market are holding on to the internet rights of their films in the hope that the internet market develops and becomes a growing area of revenue.

As foreign is still largely an area where US filmmakers do not readily venture, the sales agent who specializes in foreign is a missing link which filmmakers need to understand and work with. They have relationships built up over time and product with over 80 countries covering film licensing rights – theatrical, DVD, TV etc. An understanding of these foreign dealings is both time consuming and complex, therefore, the amateur filmmaker turned seller must be on-guard when dealing with foreign buyers. It is not impossible for a US filmmaker to become adept at selling films foreign. There are numerous examples, but in general, it is not advisable to enter that domain. Instead, leave it to a foreign sales agent professional. To assist the filmmaker with this task, I refer to my extensive section in this book entitled "selling", which will go over in detail the world of sales agents and how they may help film sales and what to be careful of. Foreign distribution/foreign revenue can mean major $$$'s!

In all this discussion about distribution and how the internet is changing the world, do not as a filmmaker forget how important the foreign territories are to your films potential revenue stream. Some 60-80% of an independent film's revenue can and often does, come from foreign sales. Foreign is very important to an independent filmmaker but it is also the hardest for a USA filmmaker to understand - let alone go after and obtain such sales in foreign territories. Sales, especially to TV, in foreign countries can be a major revenue earner for small films. Add on DVD sales and together with other platforms, foreign can be a major part of your film's revenue. Make sure as a filmmaker you do not ignore foreign. Often a good foreign sales agent is your route to the sales of TV and DVD in foreign countries. Studios certainly are aware of foreign sales in the overall income stream of their films so make sure you are!!

ONLINE DISTRIBUTION – SOME COMMENTS

There are many definitions of what online distribution really is! As technology changes so will the areas requiring some form of definition to assist in licensing agreements between parties. Online distribution may be identified as any system that delivers program content (film) by way of downloading or streaming directly to computers, households or handheld devices.

It is important to understand that online distribution is changing daily as new and interesting aspects of this technology become available and the rights issues change in the complexion. It may be worth clearly trying to understand whether to split digital rights between distributors that license downloads compared to those that stream. It is a complex area that requires attention and expert advice if the revenue amounts become significant. Some areas that require attention are:

➤ **Territory Restrictions/Holdbacks**

It is not unusual to ask for worldwide rights, however, technology is available to provide blocking capabilities to limit territory access. Language control can also help protect territory boundaries.

➤ **Exclusivity/Windows**

Exclusivity in the online distribution world appears not to be a real issue. A nonexclusive online license for a limited time would appear optimal. This would allow you to observe how the online market is maturing and provide you with future flexibility with your windows. It is also very helpful to ensure the online distributor provides a cross link from the distributor's website to the film's official website and ensure your website can sell the film also.

➤ **Materials/Delivery**

There will obviously be a delivery requirement of a digital/HD master of the film and trailer, plus other marketing materials that will benefit the sale of the film.

➤ **Sales**

One thing that will be difficult to obtain is any real idea of sales estimates. Unlike traditional rights and the potential revenue from them, the online distribution world is so new and developing distributors will not provide such estimates.

➤ **The Future - Platforms Galore!**

- A movie can be offered in 250 digital formats.

- In addition to traditional DVD, studios now have downloading or streaming to PC's, gaming consoles, iPods and other portable devices. (Xbox, PlayStation, VOD, etc.)
- Changes of Business Model - Many titles launch on cable, satellite VOD, web based download sell through, rental services and physical DVD simultaneously. The DVD head start, 15/30 day window, is rapidly changing.
- Studios introducing a multi-platform digital master format (IMF) for a movie will cover many platforms.

12 THINGS TO CONSIDER WHEN SELECTING A DISTRIBUTOR

1) Amount of advance.
2) Extent of rights conveyed. Domestic and/or foreign. Ancillary rights? Are any markets cross-collateralized?
3) Is there a guaranteed marketing commitment?
4) Does the producer have any input or veto power over artwork and theater selection in the top markets?
5) Track record and success of the distributor.
6) Are monthly or quarterly accounting statements required? Termination?
7) To what extent does the distributor plan to involve the filmmakers in promotion?
8) Marketing strategy? - demographics of intended market, grassroots promotion efforts, film festivals, etc.
9) Distribution fee? Split of revenues and accounting of profits. Overhead fees?
10) Distributor leverage with exhibitors - Can the distributor collect monies owed?
11) Any competing films handled by distributor? Conflicts of interest? Cross-collateralization of your film?
12) Does the producer have the right to regain distribution rights if the distributor pulls the plug early on distribution?

THE HITS & THE BOMBS!

- ➤ **Sex Lies & Videotape**
  Cost $1.2m / US BO $24.7m
- ➤ **Blair Witch**
  Cost $30-60k / World BO $ 249m
- ➤ **American Graffiti**
  Cost $0.75m / US BO $55m
- ➤ **Pulp Fiction**
  Cost $8.2m / US BO $108m
- ➤ **The Full Monty**
  Cost $4m / US BO $46m
- ➤ **Napoleon Dynamite**
  Cost $400k / World BO $46m
- ➤ **Battlefield Earth** (John Travolta, 2000)
  Cost $73m / US BO $21m
- ➤ **Heaven's Gate** (1980)
  Cost $40m / US BO $3.5m
- ➤ **Ishtar** (1987)
  Cost $55m / US BO $14m

EXAMPLES - MARKETING/DISTRIBUTION APPROACHES

❖ **"Nice Guy Johnny"**

Ed Burns the actor/ writer/ director made a film for $25,000 - shot it in 10 days with a digital camera with largely unknown actors on a tiny budget. His philosophy for getting the film to the audience besides utilizing websites, blogs and social networking, competitions, TV personal appearances and being a Tribeca Film festival entrant was to distribute the film via was the following:

- Video on Demand
- ITunes
- DVD
- Hulu
- Amazon
- TV sale down the road

There was no theatrical, no exclusive DVD release, no direct to TV; but, utilizing word of mouth plus limited marketing dollars to distribute the film in an online distribution model plus usual DVD approach and then TV sale.

❖ **"Blair Witch Project"**

A brilliant job of marketing and distributing a truly low, low budget feature film.

➢ *The Film Itself*
- No budget
- No music
- No script
- No stars
- No director
- No special affects
- No violence/sex
- Film style appealed to the younger generation
  Traditional marketing vs. Grass roots marketing!

➢ *Background and Production*
- Creators: Daniel Myrick and Eduardo Sanchez
- Initial costs: $30,000
- Shown at Sundance Film Festival where it was signed by Artisan Entertainment for $1 million.
- You never see anything horrible. You just see young kids who are scared to death and it worked for the movie.
- The jerk of a video camera provides the reality aspect.

➢ *Marketing Strategies*
- Create the illusion that the story is real.
- Generate hype, but not too much hype.

➢ *Website: www.blairwitch.com*
- Launched in June 1998.
- Pretended the story was real.
- Added outtakes from "discovered" film reels.
- Posted fake historical text, police reports.
- Weekly updates, new information from the story added.
- The website was an entertainment experience in itself.

➢ *Initial Target Market*
- Instead of broadcasting to the passive masses, targeted "small, rabid and influential clique that might seek out a witchy internet site".

- Results - Fans set up hypertext links between various sites, as well as to other film and occult sites.
> *Independent Film Channel (IFC)*
  - "Split Screen" program aired a short documentary spot of Blair Witch to generate interest.
  - This show gives an inside look on independent moviemaking.
> *Artisan Entertainment – Distributor*
  - John Hegeman and Gary Rubin, Artisan marketing heads, contributed $15 million for marketing and distribution.
  - Wanted to remain below the radar so it wouldn't register as hype.
  - Tie-ins for books and TV specials.
  - Blitzkrieg campaigns on college campuses.
  - Commercial merchandise, including a soundtrack CD.
> *SciFi Channel*
  - Artisan and SciFi jointly financed a special on the Blair Witch legend.
  - "Curse of the Blair Witch" aired the Monday before the movie's opening day.
  - Contained interviews with friends and relatives of the missing students, paranormal experts, and local historians.
  - It was the channels highest-rated special ever.
> *General*
  - "Anti- hype"
  - Simply showed a blurry shot, a scream, and a creepy stick figure.
  - Leaked the trailer to websites "Ain't-It-Cool-News" and MTVnews.
  - Went to 40 or so college campuses across the US and handed out missing person fliers right before school let out.
  - Creates buzz when people go home for summer.
> *Result...*
  - Released in 1999.
  - Earned $48 million in its first week of wide release.
  - The highest profit-to-cost ratio of a motion picture ever.

****

CASE STUDY:
"SERENITY FARM"
FROM INCEPTION TO SCREEN
The journey of making an ultra-low budget
independent feature film - 2011

Back in the summer of 2010, I was in discussion with a number of people in Washington State who expressed a sincere interest in being involved and contributing to the making of a feature film in the area of the Olympic Mountains two hours west of Seattle. This is the same area as the setting of the "Twilight" books.

I had already written a short synopsis of a potential feature a year or so earlier, entitled "Serenity Farm" set in this area. The story was a thriller/ horror genre utilizing the majestic locations of the local mountains and forests. Plus it incorporated the scary, never before filmed for a feature, miles of scary concrete tunnels and bunkers of an old fort with gun batteries built into the sea cliffs protecting the Puget Sound.

The following are some of the areas that I wish to pass on to filmmakers that I hope will interest readers and provide insight as to the process I went through from the summer of 2010 till July 2011, which is the time this book went to publish. As you will see at the time of this book being published we had just finished shooting and were beginning editing... For ease of explanation, I have clearly sectioned my many comments and views to help you gain a true insight into the "screen to inception" process of making an ultra-low budget film in 2010 from my own perspective.

Opening Comment: In filmmaking 101 it is generally stated that if you wish to make a really low, low budget independent feature film that is easy to produce, cheap and can be commercially successful, take a number of good looking teens, put them in a house and slaughter them in interesting ways! Why is that a good idea for a first time filmmaker? The horror genre sells all over the world; target market is young people who love this kind of genre; can shoot in one location, save costs/time; no need for any named actors so use cheap good looking talent;

shooting it in a dark scary way helps in the lack of technical ability the filmmaker has, etc. So "Serenity Farm" meets some of those elements, but as you will see, things become much more involved. I have executive produced many films and have been very involved in production on many. But this film proved to be extremely challenging. In fact, I utilized a phrase "3 dimensional chess" for the unique difficulties I encountered trying to produce and shoot this movie!

Story/Genre: Initially, I directed the tone of the story to be more horror less thriller. Later in the development process and with discussion with my TV distribution friends and the director, the script was adjusted to bring in more thriller aspects but still maintain a strong scary, terror aspect. I wanted to ensure my TV version of the film was more thriller as I know that TV revenue, especially in foreign, could be significant compared to DVD. So, bottom line, to accentuate the commercial potential of TV, more thriller was incorporated into the script.

Marketing/Commerciality: It was important that the story and how I envisioned the film, was to be commercially acceptable to the distribution buyers, especially in foreign, as I was anticipating the majority of the revenue to come from foreign TV and DVD. I, therefore, went to the AFM in November 2010 to discuss the film with my foreign distribution friends (sold many films to them over many years when I was a sales agent). In general they were very responsive to the project and that made me feel comfortable that if I produced a decent film based on my story that they would buy it.

It is a necessity to produce a quality website that includes a promo trailer, artwork, great graphics, story information, location information, bios, etc. and use this not only for potential distribution but also to attract investors and also to help you attract talent and crew.

Script: I was not going to move forward with producing this film unless I had a good script that was reflective of my synopsis. I decided to give the story to three screenwriters and see what they would come up with. Each writer I collaborated with over a three month period and was so happy to see one of the scripts was indeed very good.

Collaboration: It was important to the success of the shoot that the "set" was a happy set, as many people were working for back-end compensation and some were donating considerable time and keeping a 'normal' job going. The whole shoot was indeed a fun place and that helped with long days during filming. It was also important that the cast and the crew were from many different backgrounds and locations. This included students from Washington State universities and also local school districts. The combination of local people, local businesses, Seattle people, LA cast and crew, school kids, students, Florida cast, pro's and amateur's, local and out of state, young and old, etc. was indeed a organizational headache – but, benefitted the film greatly.

It was of great benefit to be associated with the local school district and to assist that district in providing a student class to study the filmmaking process on set. This collaboration also allowed us access to the non-profit status that helped save on costs and opened doors of mutual benefit.

Financing: Once I had a good script, I had to think about funding this film. I reviewed in detail all the many ways of funding films (see my section on film financing) and decided that I wanted to maintain full control and decided that a film like this can be made with a small amount of cash. If people would join me in making a film that no upfront fees were paid, they would share in the revenue once all my hard cash investment was paid back. On that principal I felt I could fund the cash and see how my business model would sit with crew, cast, etc. If it did, then we would have a movie that would go into production.

I presented to all concerned the formula below, for back-end/future payment that was based on a % of adjusted gross of the film's sales. Everyone who works on the film gets an agreed % of the adjusted gross which would come into play once I got back my investment.

- *Adjusted Gross* - defined as gross receipts less costs and expenses.
- *Gross Receipts* - defined as all monies, revenue and income actually received from the exploitation of the Picture from all sources worldwide.
- *Costs and Expenses* - defined as any and all direct or indirect out of pocket costs and expenses incurred by producer in connection with and without limitation, all costs incurred in the exploitation, development, pre-production, production , post-production,

marketing, publicity, advertising, promotion and distribution and selling of the Picture.

In virtually all cases this was acceptable to crew, cast, etc. This allowed me to attempt to fund this film myself and at the same time hold down costs to a minimum. Limiting costs to a bare minimum (no fees for cast or crew and reduce other costs to minimum also) is the essence of this film financing model as this will allow the adjusted gross formula to yield fees from a small number of sales.

Distribution: The one important element in all this film producing process was the fact that I had many years of selling films, both in the USA and around the world; therefore, I could guarantee distribution, especially in the foreign market, where I knew this film could do very well - if made correctly. This fact proved to be very important in attracting people to this project as they could see that there was indeed a good chance that this film would be sold around the world and that fees could be paid on the back-end per the business model outlined.

Note: The vast majority of low budget independent films that are made never get distribution, never see the light of day, never recoup their investment and deferrals are never paid.

Director/DP: It was very important to attract a quality director with the right personality type and with enough experience to be an integral part of this project. Luckily, I have worked in the film industry for many years and I knew someone who could fit that description. I meet him at the AFM and presented my film model and he agreed to do it. As always in the film business it is who you know and this relationship proved invaluable.

Cast: It is important to get professional actors. They may be in SAG or SAG eligible or with good non-union experience. I have usually hired LA actors in the past and this I did for two on the important roles; but, I branched out to Florida and I wanted Seattle based actors also. I also found three actors in the local community who really contributed greatly to the project. All agreed to the business formula. With actors from all over the USA it became an issue on flights and time schedule. Flights became a major cost. Needing to become a SAG ultra-low budget signatory, I found the complexities for such a small film as this were significant. Also, having an effective website that visually explained the film and provided cast and crew with a positive impression of the project was very important.

Crew: Obviously, quality crew became an issue as I was two hours away from Seattle. Once again I turned to my professional friends in LA to provide the director and DP. Having both a limited number of pro actors and pro director/DP made the world of difference to the quality of this film, but the costs of travel and hotels sent the costs up. I utilized film students in a major way. They were so very helpful and hardworking and they learned a lot from the pro's too – mutually beneficial. One thing I was missing in the first days of shoot was a 1st AD. We found him later in the shoot and that really helped. I utilized a number of local people for crew positions. What they did not know about the film job they made up for in tremendous effort and will.

Shoot: I decided not to shoot the film in one continuous set of days but instead break it up. In fact, we broke the shooting into four main segments. This increased the travel costs. The total shoot was 24 days, split into four main shooting periods (May7-9; June 11-14; June25 - July3; July13-19 and two days in LA). Our main shoot period was a nine day, 16 hours a day shoot, covering three locations with one hour travel apart. Having breaks in shooting was very important, especially as I was using crew that had other jobs and they were volunteering time to do the film. Without that they would not have been able to help on the film. This was also beneficial as it allowed us to see the good and the bad of what we were doing and make adjustments, especially on how the crew was doing their jobs and of course how the film clips looked.

From a logistical perspective we had over 5000 video clips. These clips ranged in length from 8 seconds to 8 minutes, with an average probably around 60-75 seconds each, from our multiple cameras. This produces about 95 hours of footage. This does not include the GoPro footage or the behind the scenes footage, which will add another 15-20 hours of material. Good luck to our editor!

Locations: The film locations were two hours west of Seattle so getting people there was a challenge. We basically used four locations, namely the farm, a small town and the two bunker/ tunnel forts. Locations were one hour drive from each other. Getting permits for state parks proved challenging indeed. The cost of locations proved to be minimal, which is very different from LA. Local people were so helpful.

Time of year: The film could be set any time of year but due to our schedule we shot in May/June/July 2011. However, we did some shooting in winter to help with rain/storms. From a cost perspective (flight/hotels), since it was summer and this area is a tourist haven, those costs rose. On the plus side, the weather made it pleasant for shooting.

Accommodations: To help keep costs down a number of the crew and other local people generously provided accommodations to crew and actors during the shoot. This was a major cost saving as we had a large number from outside the area that needed to be put up.

Equipment: We used the Sony EX1 HD camera – often using three or four of them - a quality work horse of a camera. Our director owned one so it was an easy decision to go that way. All my films in the past have been on 35mm so shooting on digital HD was interesting. I still needed to ensure the quality was there, as I always respect the need for quality when selling films to foreign TV stations. Renting cameras and lights can cost serious money but great people helped so much by lending use their equipment... A big thank you to them!

Filmmakers make a big note - foreign TV stations require a high level of technical quality on feature films.

Website/Internet: Naturally we produced an official website (www.serenityfarmthemovie.com). We also generated information and engagement via my website and via Facebook. I also realized that the film sales were not going to come via internet traffic, in whatever form, but from my expertise in film sales agency. One thing I tried was crowd funding. I set up a project on "kickstarter.com" to see how the whole process worked. I quickly realized that to be successful a great deal of time is required to attract donations from individuals. I did not have that time but it is certainly a new and exciting funding potential avenue.

Note: A point of interest to filmmakers is the way I used a promo of the upcoming film production. To help me market the film to potential distributors I shot a short promo of the locations and have a voice over telling the story. I used local actors and went to the three locations and shot a short promo of the story. Besides using this promo to create a visual impression of the story to distributors I also used it to help build up the website into a marketing tool that I used to entice and attract actors, crew and director, etc. This proved to be highly effective and, along with my explaining how I was to produce this film and the financing aspects, I was able to put this film together.

Post-Production: We are about to finish the production phase of the film and move into editing. Having a detailed work flow and logging of clips is vital. Also ensure you have all material backed up and stored off site from your editor. Our editor works in the following manner:

1) Bins for each scene.

2) Within scenes there are folders for wide shoots, close- ups, medium.

3) Bins for each b-roll within each scene.

4) Separate bins for things such as weather, tunnel, animals, rivers, oceans, creatures, skyline.

Editing is a long process and requires detail. Both the director and myself will be heavily involved. Music will come soon and again this part is so vital to the success of the film. Based on how things are going this film should be completed by the end of 2011.

Summary: This whole film comes down to balancing the need for quality (both in cast and crew) compared to paying out hard cash up front. My vision was and still is to produce a quality product for such a small amount of cash up front, that when I sell two or three territories I will recoup my investment. Then all film members (crew and cast) will share in the revenues. This business model seems to make sense to me in these times. In addition, I control the film 100% because I know (hopefully I know!) what sells and how to sell it, especially to foreign territories, where the majority of the film revenue will come.

To all the cast and crew of "Serenity Farm"...
"Say no more" and "Bob's your uncle"

****

SELLING

HIGHLIGHTS OF THIS CHAPTER...

*GOOD NEWS/BAD NEWS ABOUT
SELLING YOUR FILM!*

HOW MUCH IS YOUR FILM WORTH?

WHAT IS A SALES AGENT?

*SALES AGENT AGREEMENT —
POINTS TO WATCH*

PRE-SALES — WHAT YOU NEED TO KNOW

SALES AGENTS - TRICKS OF THE TRADE

WHAT IS A PRODUCER'S REP?

WHAT IS A BUYER'S REP?

FILM MARKETS

FILM FESTIVALS

*THINGS YOU SHOULD KNOW ABOUT
SELLING YOUR OWN FILM*

SELLING
"THE GOOD, THE BAD AND THE UGLY"

GOOD NEWS/BAD NEWS...... ABOUT SELLING YOUR FILM!

❖ **Bad News** - The majority of independent feature films never really see the light of day. In 2008 Sundance Film Festival had over 3500 submissions. Just over 120 got accepted. Only 2 got any kind of distribution.

❖ **Good News** - One or two make buckets of money.

WHAT IS SELLING?

Selling is offering to exchange something of value for something else. To be a seller you must have a buyer! Selling is often thought to be part of marketing, but the skills to sell are very different – hence, why I have designated a separate chapter entitled "Selling" and another entitled "Marketing".

HOW DO WE SELL A FILM?

Firstly, you need to understand what you have in your 120k feet of 35 mm film or on hard drive/ HD content. You have intellectual property. That's what you have – not a car, fridge or a widget, something physical that you can touch and move around your house – but, intellectual property. Therefore, intellectual property for the purposes of sales agents is **licensed** - not sold in the way of car sales. You need to know that any licensing contract for your film covers four areas and you need to understand them. These four areas are:

1) *Rights* - the inherent elements of your property (Theatrical, TV, DVD, etc.)
2) *Territory* – the physical area concerned (USA, Germany, UK, etc.)
3) *Term* – the time period you are licensing the film (number of years)
4) *Value* – the $$$$ you get for licensing your film

Make sure you understand these terms as you will badly screw up if you are not clear. An example of a simple film licensing deal done by a foreign sale agent would be a film, 94 minutes long, titled "Tons of

Fun" and it is being licensed for the territory of Germany, for 15 years, for all TV, for a license fee of $150,000.

HOW MUCH IS YOUR FILM WORTH?

Depends on many factors the following being some of them:

- ➤ **The Story/The Film Genre:** A good script and story helps. That story being in a marketable genre also helps. Genre means it has a clear slot in the public's mind in that it is a family film or an action film or a horror film, etc. Plus genre tends to go in commercial waves, like romantic comedies can be in one year and out the next.
- ➤ **The Package:** The actors, the director and the script. Naturally, in the independent low budget world Brad Pitt is rarely available to you as a producer so settle for the best talent you can find at the best price for your available funds. You will be surprised who you can attract, especially if the script is good. The better the actor with some form of film credentials the more attractive to the buyers. Or a director of some note – (eg. Frank Henenlotter is known purely as a niche horror director of some note) can help you sell the film to distributors around the world.
- ➤ **The Budget:** The budget. What is the budget? Usually the larger the budget the more the sales. This is not necessarily so. I remember representing a $2m budget film that generated fewer sales than my own financed $750k film. Certain budgets demand certain needs in distribution. At some point, if the budget gets larger, a theatrical release will be expected and that has its own concerns and difficulties. Some budgets are not large enough for theatrical, but are too big for the revenues generated from all the other rights to cover the budget – any bag of concerns. Generally in low budget films, the vast majority of your sales will come from TV and DVD and the majority of revenue will come from foreign.
- ➤ **Production Value and Quality:** This area involving your film can be elevated way above its station. Ensuring good production value and quality sound and picture can really help low budget films to maximize sales. Similarly, if those values are low, sales will follow.
- ➤ **Timing:** Timing can be very important. I remember as a sales agent, I had a buyer come to my AFM office and they wanted to buy three dramas with B actors that had not been sold in the major

territories and were immediately available to buy outright. Well, I just had three waiting for such an offer. The deal was done in minutes. The films delivered and we collected a big chunk of $$$$$'s – now that is timing! Similarly, film genres get hot for a period of time - Horror for a year or so - then action films were hot... Genre "hotness" comes and goes. Certainly, I found family films to always be in demand and sold all over the world.

➤ **Theatrical or Not:** Wow! – This is a good discussion topic and open to debate. Certainly, if the film has a larger budget, then a theatrical release might be needed to try and boost the prices from DVD and TV that would be too low if no theatrical occurred. However, going theatrical might not have any effect. Then, if the numbers are not good – you just wasted money! What kind of release do you think is right for the film and do you have the money for a release? Many questions with many options including no theatrical - period.

A theatrical release of substance (not just one or two) can and does have a significant influence on potential sales. A successful release in the USA is not only good for US sales but also has a major impact on international revenue. There are numerous forms of release, but suffice to say, that a meaningful release can be very beneficial to sales.

➤ **Sales Estimates:** Often an experienced sales agent can provide the producer with reasonably detailed sales estimates (good, expected, low), especially on foreign. This can help guide a producer on the films revenue potential/worth. These estimates will provide an idea of the films worth, less of course the sales agent's fee and all expenses!

WHAT IS A SALES AGENT?

Let us begin by clearly stating the difference between a distributor and a sales agent. A distributor takes your film and distributes your product directly to the consumer. A sales agent is an agent. He represents your film in order to find a distributor to license your film and distribute it. A sales agent is very much like a real estate broker trying to find a buyer for your property. An agent needs to ensure the film is marketed correctly and is presented to the right buyers for your type of product. Sales agents are often international sales agents, but may also be domestic as well as international agents. These agents will license your film (completed or not) on a territory by territory basis through the world. The primary task is to sell your film to theatrical distributors (if possible), television companies, home video/ DVD companies and others. In most cases a sales agent is just that - an agent in making distribution deals. The distribution rights of the film which are part of the copyright in the film are not transferred. For these services an agent charges a fee and recoups incurred costs.

Once a film is sold, the distributor or sales agent negotiates the contracts and finalizes the terms and conditions. Agents are then responsible for delivering all the required elements of the film to the distributor. Finally, the agent will also be the collection agent for the money transactions involved in the deal and hopefully any profit. Then the agent will disperse the monies based on the sales agent's contract deal terms. Agents must also provide regular financial accountings for client filmmakers, which will include a breakdown of costs and income for each film.

Sales agents need to continually acquire new films in order to keep their film libraries/catalogues fresh and up to date for potential buyers. Agents, therefore, continually hunt for new and exciting product. They attend screenings and festivals, meet with new filmmakers and network within the industry. Sales agents must promote their new films at various film festivals and film markets, provide DVD copies of the films for potential buyers and, of course, keep in contact with the many buyers both domestically and internationally to keep abreast of buyers needs and requirements. Sales agents constantly communicate with buyers to ensure they are fully up to date on film trends and requirements of buyers, especially what types of films are selling, which genres, which actors, etc.

Agents are also responsible for brokering deals for filmmakers, unless they employ their own legal advisors. Agents usually work with delivery services, which dispatch all the necessary materials to distributors. Because films are sold to a large number of territories, this work is ongoing. Agents must also provide regular financial accounts for client filmmakers, including a breakdown of costs and income for each film. Sales agents also know which buyers actually pay on time or cause delays or anything else relevant to the financial capabilities of the buyers.

THE MISSING LINK!

Another important function of sales agents is in the realm of film financing. The ability of assisting a filmmaker to obtain film funding before the film goes into production is a very important aspect of a sales agent. I view this as a missing link that producers need to be aware of and understand. It may provide a final link to their financing and, as such, get the film funded and into production. More about this later...

WHAT DOES A SALES AGENT DO ... AND CAN THIS HELP YOU?

- ➢ Find a buyer/distributor for your film – domestically and/or internationally.
- ➢ Provide marketing expertise and possibly marketing funds to help sell your movie.
- ➢ Provide expertise and knowledge about the film buying market - both domestically and internationally. Knowing which buyers to approach with your type of film product.
- ➢ Provide expertise in knowing/understanding sales pricing, terms, conditions and availability for your product.
- ➢ Provide the ability for your product to be represented at the various film markets and film festivals around the world and to be professionally displayed to buyers.
- ➢ Negotiate and provide industry expertise with potential sales contracts.
- ➢ Provide expertise in delivery requirements of buyers, especially internationally.
- ➢ Assist in providing funds for production financing and/or provide pre-sales contracts for funding. Knowledge and experience in

dealing with entertainment banks can also be provided by a sales agent in funding said contracts.

➢ Provide general expertise and experience in assisting producers with banks regarding production funding. Certain sales agents can also provide sales estimates that financial institutions may use to help provide gap financing in a film production situation.

➢ Provide a liaison service between producer and buyer.

FIND A SALES AGENT

I always think it sad when a producer finishes his film, signs on a sales agent and then waits for months and hears nothing. What is worse - gets no money from any sales. To help mitigate this, a producer must use some common sense and be on guard for an agent who does not fit with his needs or hopes.

How does one select a good sales agent? Well this is not easy. Start by finding out who are the sales agents. Do this by obtaining a copy of the Hollywood Distribution Directory, published by the Hollywood Reporter. The link is: www.shophcdonline.com

This directory is a great source of information. Select a few and check them out. Look at the type of films they represent; how long have they been in business; do they attend film markets; can they provide references; ask friends in the film biz if they know of them - do due diligence.

The Independent Film and Television Alliance (IFTA — formerly AFMA) is also an excellent source of information and assistance. IFTA is the independent sales agents' trade organization that organizes the American Film Market every year in Santa Monica and provides many benefits to its members and the film community.

HOW TO FIND AND EVALUATE A SALES AGENT

Do your homework. Do research and ask questions. Selecting an agent that works for you is very important. One, you will have to work with them for a long time; two, they are your avenue to get your film investment back. Believe me I have seen many producers/filmmakers sign the wrong agent and suffer much grief because of it. Remember "swimming with sharks" is not just a fancy saying - it is true.

Firstly, talk to friends in the film business, read articles, call the AFMA, talk to friends who have made and sold films for their recommendations.

Secondly, research websites from the list of sales agents you have obtained and look at the type of films they sell, etc. and how long they have been in business, etc. and do background checks. Many sales agents represent many genres and types of film with differing budget levels, so make sure that if your film is ultra-low with no name actors that the company deals in that type of film.

Thirdly, check out if the company you are interested in will provide an upfront guarantee or finishing money should your film need finishing. This can often tip the scales to who you will sign with.

Believe me you will find out which sales agents to avoid!

SALES AGENTS – "SWIMMING WITH SHARKS"!

I have titled this section, sales agents - "swimming with sharks", after the film about film agents starring Kevin Spacey. If you haven't seen it, go watch it! It is a great representation of what goes on in the film biz and what an actor's agent is like.

Sales agents are truly an important element of the independent film world. Yet so little is known or understood by a large portion of the independent filmmakers of the world, especially outside of Los Angeles. How many of you can name one independent sales agent? What do they do? How can they help you? So let's discuss about the good, the bad and the ugly of film sales agents. There is plenty of all these attributes, but with a bit of help you might learn how to avoid some of the pitfalls in dealing with this animal!!!

Before we move forward, let us discuss desperation! Desperation plays a huge part of the film world - desperation to get the funding, desperation to get the actors, locations, etc. But, once the shoot is finished desperation doesn't end. You need to pay for your film to get money back to your Dad or to an investor or just to yourself after two years of hard grueling work. I have been there – more than once, let me tell you how I did it.

Also, let me tell you that I am and have for over twenty years been a sales agent in Hollywood, in the independent film industry, so my comments are coming from practical and lived through experience from both sides, which I know will benefit you.

CAN A SALES AGENT REALLY HELP?

A sales agent is usually contracted by the producer of a film as agent to arrange the selling of the distribution rights of the film to domestic and foreign distributors. An agent for these services will charge a fee based on the sales price of the deals. A sales agent is an important link between a filmmaker and the actual final consumer. A distributor takes on the responsibility of selling/licensing the film to its various markets, including theatrical, DVD, TV and so on to the consumer. Understanding the distinction and what these statements mean is really important to a producer who wants to get his film seen by the general public because these agents and distributors can make your dreams happen – but at a price!!

Sales agents can and do act as agents to sell rights both to domestic distributors and foreign distributors; however, they are most known for selling rights in the foreign territories and hence, they are more commonly known as foreign sales agents. Why are they more common dealing with foreign countries is obvious? Most filmmakers in the US are not experts in dealing with the rest of the world. Knowledge and understanding of the foreign market is very necessary in dealing with international buyers (whether foreign TV networks or foreign DVD distributors). Often US filmmakers know more about their own back yard and feel they can go directly to US distributors to sell their product. Although that can be a bad mistake as most filmmakers are not experts on sales, marketing and distribution deals - let alone knowing how to approach or contact the right people at the US distribution companies.

HOW A SALES AGENT CAN HELP? - MARKETING

In the area of marketing your film, sales agents can really help the producer and even prepare and promote the sales and marketing materials for the film. At an early stage of a script and film package (actor, director, etc.) a sales agent can help the producer in knowing what genres sell best around the world, what kind of script, what kind of actors, what budget level and what revenues can be expected. This is very valuable advice, as so many filmmakers write or produce films and they have no idea whether their film project has any commerciality. Why make a film that has no chance of making a profit or even getting the investor's money back? So many films are made just like that.

Often I would ask a producer/filmmaker about his film - "Why did you make it?" If the answer is I love it, then good, but don't cry on me as a sales agent when I cannot sell it and your investors lose money! It amazes me that so many filmmakers have little idea about the potential commercialization of their film and where there is a market for their product. To spend so much time, effort and love on a film to find it cannot be sold is very sad. Sales agents also have a lot of experience in what sells and the marketing tools associated with that - namely, posters, artwork, trailers, and press kits. In many cases the sales agent will pay for such materials and recoup later once revenue comes in.

HOW IMPORTANT ARE THE MARKETING MATERIALS?

Trailers and posters are very important tools for the sales agent. They can most certainly make or break a sale to a buyer. Having good effective artwork and a compelling trailer are so important. A sales agent should possess the experience and knowledge required to ensure both the trailer and artwork have the most effective elements included to help appeal to the buyers. Depending on the genre of the film and the package included, the following points can be made:

➤ **Sell Sheet/Poster** – Probably the foremost marketing tool available to you as a filmmaker. An intriguing and compelling poster can attract buyers and raise interest in your film. Such posters can and do help sell your film whether your film is complete or just in pre-production. A great selling tool and, in such, can generate money from a license deal or as a fund raising tool.

A sell sheet/poster or rather the artwork should reflect the genre, tone and content of the film. Such artwork should be clear, compelling and arouse the interest of the viewer, whether it be a buyer or a member of the general public.

There are a number of elements involved in the creation process of posters:

- *The Key Art* - The main visual component of the poster.
- *The Title Treatment* - The font, style and look of the film title.
- *Copy* – Actors names, director, reviews, etc.
- *Billing* – Formal rules regarding the film credits.
- *Layout* - The general look, positioning and feel of the whole poster.
- *Taglines* – The short few words that catch the essence of the film and what it is about.

Some more tips to help create an effective sell sheet are:

- Must be eye catching, four color and attractive, but also reflect the nature of the film.
- The graphics should be clear and attention grabbing.
- Use clear type fonts and color schemes for film title, credits and taglines.
- Any actors or director of note, ensure their names are prominent.
- Use the back cover for text/synopsis about the film and have photos of scenes from the film. Plus all contact information must be clearly identified.
- Use good quality paper with quality printing – cardboard stock.

As a filmmaker/producer one has a number of choices regarding the creation of a poster. You can always hire a graphic artist to create the poster for you and the cost can be relatively low; or, you can wait till you get a sales agent to do it for you. I have found that a poster is of great benefit in film fund raising activities as it gives people/investors the feel that the project is real!

Often a sales agent will develop their own poster for the film as they are the experts and they wish to portray the film as they see it from their marketing perspective. Once the film is licensed to international buyers it is not unusual to have one or more countries totally revamp the poster to fit their own marketing needs and that might also include changing the film's title.

➢ **Trailers – teaser or regular** (see marketing section) - Trailers are another important marketing tool for your film. Effective trailers are a must and there is definitely an art in producing trailers.

➢ **Trade Ads** – Film ads in the trade papers - eg. Variety
➢ **Press Kits/EPKs (electronic press kits)** – A very important marketing tool. EPK's go to: TV stations, press, cinemas, DVD stores, buyers, etc. They can include the following:
  - *Featurette* (25 min. behind the scenes/interviews)
  - *Trailer* (Teaser/regular)
  - *B-Roll Footage* (Informal footage during filming)
  - *Sound Bites* (Cast answering question from interviewer – off camera)
  - *Short Newsy Stories*
  - *TV Clips* (TV coverage of film)
  - *Music Video/Soundtrack*
  - *Poster/Artwork*

SALES AGENT AGREEMENT - POINTS TO WATCH

In my many years of being an active sales agent, my company has always had licensing contracts written between my company and the distributor, whether it be for foreign or domestic. The producer is not included in the contract terms. All contract matters were between my company and the company licensing the film. I know that other companies and producers have had contracts between the producer and the distributor directly and the sales agent does the negotiating.

Usually, as sales agent, we would exchange potential deal points. Once agreed upon, a formal deal memo would be exchanged and then a long form licensing contract would be drawn up and ultimately signed by both parties – the sales agent and the distributor.

A contract between a producer and sales agent is an important and complex document. If it is not fully examined it can cause the producer real heartache over a long period of time. So try and do it right up front and pay for a good entertainment lawyer to help you!

Remember, the primary task is to sell your film to theatrical distributors (if possible), television companies, home video/DVD companies and others. An agent will find a distributor, then negotiate and document the deal terms and conditions for the film. In most cases a sales agent is just that, an agent in making distribution deals.

The distribution rights of the film, which are part of the copyright in the film, are not transferred.

➢ **Form of Contract:** Producers should ensure that the sales agent uses the standard Independent Film and Television Alliance (IFTA) deal memos for licensing. Often long form contracts tend to vary, but do ensure you approve the deal memo and the long form format.

➢ **Rights:** A sales agent normally will be licensing all rights pertaining to the film. Be certain you wish the sales agent to sell all rights or where you wish internet rights or other rights to be excluded.

➢ **Territory:** Which territories worldwide does the sales agent have approval to sell to? Usually agents represent the world, including the USA/Canada, or just foreign. Certainly, if the sales agent has put up an advance/financing then they will want to sell the world. Certainly, in my experience I have handled both the world and only foreign. I have found that regarding USA rights I would often go to a colleague who specializes in the USA market and specializes in TV deals or DVD deals and do the deal through them. That enables me to collect a commission on a USA sale. With foreign I knew all the buyers so I went directly to them. Internet rights are another source of concern as that involves "border protection" issues that must be addressed. The IFTA can be of assistance on this matter.

➢ **Term of Contract:** A producer needs to ensure the agent has enough time to sell, but if he is not doing a great job, you need to be able to terminate. One way is to agree to a short term deal, maybe one year with the option of an additional year. Another way to try and ensure performance by the agent, is to try and state that if sales do not approach a certain amount within a period of time the producer can terminate. This area can be contentious so be prepared to negotiate.

➢ **Order of recoupment:** The order of recoupment and the allocation of net receipts between the producer and sales agent is a very important area and should be carefully reviewed as it involves MONEY!!! - And whether you get any of it!! The terms "first position" and "second position" are often used. If a bank is involved in financing they invariably gets first position from any and all sources of revenue from the sale of the film. First position means that money received by the sales agent goes first to the bank to pay off their loan. Once the bank is paid then other groups can be provided an order of recoupment allocation. Every situation is different and can be complex. It is imperative the producer fully understands where the money/receipts are being distributed and in what manner. The following example of order of recoupment comes from one of my actual producer/ ales agency agreements:

Application of Gross Receipts:

Gross Receipts shall be applied in the following order and priority

1) First, to the production lender to repay the production loan for the picture and to pay charges (including interest) and fees.

2) Second, to the completion guarantor to recoup any completion funds for the picture paid by the completion guarantor (and charges).

3) Third, to the sales agent in payment of their sales fee of 20% of all gross receipts without deduction therefrom - retroactive to the first dollar of gross receipts, plus their recoupment of distribution costs and expenses (per agreement).

4) Fourth, to the producer, any remaining earned and non-returnable gross receipts, except for a reasonable reserve for future distribution costs or expenses.

Take note that the production lender and the completion bond company get top priority in return of monies. The sales agent of course receives their sales fee/ commission plus all their approved expenses.

➤ **Approval of Sales:** This is an interesting issue and can cause many problems for both the producer and the agent. Naturally, the producer wants to maximize revenue so having sales estimates provided by the agent gives the producer an idea on such a figure. In practice, the agent will provide a list of minimum sales prices that below which the agent cannot sell without the approval of the producer. Usually, such minimums cover only the top territories. This presents two issues: Firstly, does the minimum price per a territory cover all rights (and it usually does) and what happens if you split rights for that territory? Secondly, if you are at a film market, say Cannes or even in Santa Monica, and a buyer makes an offer below the minimum and the buyer wants an answer there and then (and that does and will happen many times). The agent is bound by the contract to contact the producer to ask his OK to take the deal. This can and does present a problem if instant communication cannot be obtained. Also, there might need to be a discussion between producer and agent to make a decision. Either way, a sale could be (and has been) lost due to this limitation. I would strongly suggest you discuss these matters with the agent to provide a balance that works in practice.

➢ **Sales Commission:** This section is usually the area of major debate and negotiation between producer and sales agent. It is possible to state that if a sales agent is providing any form of financing or even pre-sales assistance to the film then the sales commission will be higher. A typical fee structure for a sales agent dealing with a completed film would be between 20% - 25% for foreign and 10%-15% for USA/Canada – variations are not uncommon such as a sliding scale based on results. These fees should be based on net receipts to the agent in the US, not on gross, as there may be taxes withheld in foreign countries.

➢ **Escrow Account:** It is reasonable to request that all gross receipts shall be paid directly to the agent and deposited into a separate segregated bank account, which the agent shall maintain for the picture. As a sales agent, I would not allow this unless the film and producer were important to me and they were insistent, as it is more of an administration hassle for the agent.

➢ **Advance:** Producers can and do ask for advance payments from sales agents on signing the agreement. I never ever gave advances. Producers feel it is an act of good faith and also faith in the film. This advance can also be used, depending on its size, to help complete a film. Naturally, should an agent give such an advance, the cost to the producer is often in higher fees and less control over the film and its sales.

➤ **Accounting:** Producers should receive quarterly statements of account and payments with respect to the picture within thirty (30) days after the end of the quarter to which such statement relates during the first two years following delivery of the picture, and semi-annually thereafter (within 60 days after the end of each such semi-annual period), with no statement required for any period during which no gross receipts are received. Also, get signed and fully executed copies of all licensing agreements with buyers on sales made for your film. The ability to audit, once a year, the sales agent's accounting records is also a reasonable item to request.

➤ **Distribution/Delivery Expenses:** This is another area that, as a producer, you must pay serious attention to. Sales agents usually have considerable expenses involving film markets and costs incurred in producing and generating marketing and sales materials. Agents will want to ensure they recoup such expenses from revenue generated from the sale of the films they handle. Producers need to be aware that expenses generally fall into two categories - namely, direct out of pocket expenses that can be clearly assigned to a film (marketing/distribution costs) and secondly, the allocated costs relating to the attendance of a film market. The direct out of pocket costs will include preparation and printing of key art, posters and advertisements, the producing of trailers, creation of press kits, generating DVD screeners for buyers and all the ancillary costs of shipping and other costs incurred with materials of your film. Often such costs with a low budget film can be in the range from $10,000 to $20,000. As a producer you should expect to see a detailed listing of such costs in your accounting from the agent.

The second category of costs namely, the allocation of film market costs, is more an area of discussion and often a bone of contention between producer and agent; but, must be settled in the sales agent agreement. Going to a film market involves many different costs that should be borne by all the films the sales agent is representing at that market. Film markets include the AFM, Cannes, Berlin etc. and these costs can be substantial. Such costs will include market exhibitor entry fees and set up fees, airfare, hotel and food cost, equipment rental, local labor assistant, telephone/fax, etc. Firstly, let me say that there is no standard way of allocation and usually the sales agent has their own method which they will present to you in the agreement. In my case, I would do it pro rata basis on the films I was representing at that market. Although it was also common that each film producer would negotiate a flat fee for each market - with a cap. An example would be $10,000 for Cannes, $10,000 for AFM and then a further $5,000 to cover Berlin and say MIPCOM - a total cap of $25,000 and that was it – no more allocated costs even if the agent went to more markets and represented the film there also. Naturally, the sales agent who was out of pocket for all these costs including the direct costs would only get their investment back from making sales of the film and collecting the license fees from buyers.

Following is a list of reimbursable distribution expenses which are normally incurred in connection with the marketing and distribution of a film:

1) Travel
2) Film Market Expenses
3) Trade Ad – Design/Printing
4) Trade Ad – Space
5) Sales Presentation Package
6) Preliminary Artwork
7) Stills and Transparencies
8) Photography and Photo Books
9) Synopsis
10) Promo Reels
11) Press Kits and Press Kit Copies
12) Master, Sub-masters and Conversion Masters
13) TV Brochures
14) Printing and Xeroxing
15) Shipping
16) Local & International Courier
17) Telephone/Faxes
18) MV Meals and Entertainment
19) Taxes and Licenses
20) Legal

21) Consularization Fees
22) Miscellaneous

➤ **Delivery:** Often producers neglect the costs involved in delivery of film elements necessary for the sale of the film. Delivery items are a negotiated item. The list can be lengthy and they have to be paid for either by the producer or the sales agent who recoups later. Foreign delivery needs usually require a PAL master and separate soundtracks for dubbing foreign languages.

The following is a generic deliverables list for a non-theatrical

feature film:

- *HD Cam SR (1080p 23.98)*
- *NTSC DBC (16X9 1:85 LBX)*
- *PAL DBC (16X9 1:85 LBX)*
- *NTSC DBC (4X3 1:85 LBX)*
- *PAL DBC (4X3 1:85 LBX)*
- *DBC PAL & NTSC -- trailer*
- *DBC EPK (PAL & NTSC)*
- *Key Art – layers/textless and texted*
- *Press kit/EPK*
- *Dialogue/Action Continuity Spotting List*
- *Production Notes*
- *Music Cue Sheet*
- *DAT Copy - musical score*
- *Certificate of Origin*
- *Certificate of Authorship*
- *Copyright Certificate*
- *Paid Advertising and Credit Obligation/Main and End Title Credits*
- *Title research report*
- *Copyright Search Report*
- *Lab Access Letters if needed*
- *Script*
- *E & O Certificate – domestic only*
- *MPAA Rating Certificate*
- *Characteristics of Picture – Running time, aspect ratio, etc.*

➤ **Cure Right:** This is a good clause to put into your agreement as it formally puts the offending party on notice of a problem. "Each party, hereto, will have 30 days from receipt of written notice from the other party, thereof, to cure any purported breach of this agreement."

➢ **Marketing Materials:** All producers should understand that the sales agent is very experienced in presenting films to the international market and, therefore, are well aware of how marketing materials, especially posters and trailers, should be prepared and look to help maximize sales. The sales agent will insist on approving all marketing materials even if you do them yourself; however, always ask for creative input.

Take note that each country will amend all the marketing materials provided due to language, culture, censorship, etc. and will, if they feel it necessary, change the title of the film itself.

➢ **Arbitration:** Make sure you have in any agreement with an agent a binding arbitration clause that, in the event of a dispute, no law courts are used to settle the matter; but, an arbitration tribunal will make a decision that is binding on all parties. This is cheaper and quicker than law courts.

➢ **Residuals:** This is another serious area and needs to be addressed in the agreement. As a sales agent I always tried to ensure that I had the producer take care of all guild residuals. These residuals related to home video and TV exploitation. Be aware that should the producer not pay such residuals and the guilds try to collect directly from sales agents, this can cause serious problems with regards to collecting on domestic sales if there are outstanding residuals due at the guilds.

➢ **Copyright/E & O:** Naturally all producers must protect the copyright of their product and the sales agent will ask for proof of copyright and ownership. In addition, E & O (Errors and Omissions) becomes an important element, only for domestic sales, where a copy of an E & O policy will be part of the delivery requirements for a domestic distributor to ensure against claims of libel, copyright infringement, etc. This is a cost that is often forgotten, but for foreign sales it is not a necessity.

➢ **Sales Estimates/Potential Revenue:** A producer should ask the agent to provide a list of potential revenues for the major territories. This usually covers <u>all rights</u> for the individual countries such as Germany, UK and Japan, etc. Such a list can be very revealing, as it will show the producer, probably for the first time, the potential revenue he may get for the film.

I attach examples of a sales agent's estimates. An example is also published in the Hollywood Reporter in the bumper issue at major film markets such as the AFM. What is beneficial about this list given to you by your potential agent is that the producer can state that territories cannot be sold beneath a set price without producer agreement. This prevents an agent selling your film below a value you wish to obtain – of course, that has its own downside also in that you need to negotiate that with the agent and they might feel inhibited during the sales process at a market. So there is good and bad in this area.

There are two traditional methods used by sales agents to provide potential prices to be obtained in the different territories. Firstly, there is the percentage of production budget method and secondly, the price range based on empirical judgment by experts in this area based on budget.

Note: As a producer, please be aware that the following percentages/figures are sales estimates and must be interpreted with extreme caution. Whether you use the budget method or the method of the sales agents' judgment, such estimates are based on many factors such as budget, timing, genre, talent, production value, etc. It is common that individual sales agents will provide different estimates. A producer should use these estimates as a guide and not as fact. Often the sales price you actually attain from a territory can be very different than the original estimate provided by the sales agent. As I have said before, these sales estimates usually incorporate all rights (not broken down by individual rights).

❖ *Percentage of Production Budget Method:*

    Schedule of expected prices per territory (% of budget)

Domestic (USA/Canada)	20 – 45%
Germany	10%

UK	8%
France	7%
Italy	4%
Spain	4%
Scandinavia	3%
Japan	10%
S. Korea	3%
Taiwan	1%
Brazil	1%
Australia/NZ	3%

❖ *Price Range Based On Empirical Judgment and Sales Agent's Experience Method:*

	Budget of films in the range:	
	Less $1m	$1–$2M
USA/Canada	$25k - 200k	$50k - 1.0m
United Kingdom	$15k - 75k	$50k - 150k
Australia/NZ	$10k - 25k	$30k - 75k
German Speaking	$15k - 100k	$50k - 200k
France	$15k - 30k	$40k - 100k
Italy	$10k - 25k	$30k - 100k
Japan	$15k - 75k	$50k - 175k
Latin America	$15k - 30k	$30k - 100k
Scandinavia	$10k - 35k	$40k - 75k
South Korea	$10k - 50k	$30k - 100k
Spain	$10k - 30k	$40k - 75k

PRE-SALES – WHAT YOU NEED TO KNOW

Pre-sales are an important aspect of being a sales agent and are little understood by independent producers. Pre-sales can be the difference between making your indie film and not, between enticing an investor to invest in your film or not.

WHAT ARE PRE-SALES?

The concept of pre-sales relates to the ability of a sales agent to present your film package (script, cast, director, etc.) to a distributor/buyer and have them commit to licensing your film before the film is completed or even before production has begun. This is a valuable asset when the producer is trying to finalize the funding of a film at whatever stage in development (pre-production, production or post) the film is in. A pre-sale can put the film into a green light position and make the project happen... A major celebration point if you are a hard working producer close to making a film.

Please understand, anyone can make a pre-sale including the producer, but you need to know the world of film sales and distribution and most of all you need to know the buyers for your type of product. Are they willing to contract with you? Here the sales agent with their experience and knowledge can step forward on behalf of the producer.

WHY WOULD YOU PRE-SELL YOUR FILM PROJECT?

One of the main reasons of a pre-sale is to obtain financing to make your film happen. Secondly, by pre-selling a territory or two, your investor(s) will take comfort with the fact that distribution companies in the film business have confidence in the commerciality of your film. These distributors, whether in the USA or foreign, are willing to pre-buy your film package and not only place a deposit (usually 20% of the minimum guarantee), but also provide an executed licensing contract that can be submitted to an entertainment bank as collateral. That bank providing cash (certain % of the balance) directly to the funding of the film production is a major plus.

PRE-SALE CONCERNS

Firstly, you have to find distributors willing to view your film package in such a positive light and make that commitment.

Secondly, the distributor must be "bankable". That means the entertainment bank you use has to feel comfortable that when the film is finished and delivered to the distributor, the distributor will pay per the contract. This area can often be a major challenge and experience and knowledge of this area is critical.

Thirdly, pre-selling involves selling territories on a film not yet released. If you sell short on a good film you might be losing possibly more revenue than if you waited till the film was released, then sell it.

Fourthly, do you really need pre-sales to finance or partly finance your film? By definition a pre-sale means that you as the producer designate certain rights of your film to the distributor, for a certain territory for a certain period of time and the distributor agrees to pay you a certain amount of money based on certain terms and conditions. Such terms usually require full delivery of the film within a certain period and that film has the agreed actors, script, budget, technical requirements, etc. Providing the distributor is "bankable" (bankable meaning credit worthy) the producer can take the contract and "bank it" with an entertainment financial institution and that contract will be the collateral for a production loan to help you cash flow your production. (Go to Film Financing section for more information on film banking) This contract can also be presented to an investor as evidence that the film is commercial. The evidence of this is that a distributor is interested enough in the merits of the film to pre-buy and so the investor will loan against the contract or have the contract provide him enough security to have him make an equity stake in the project. Usually in a pre-sale the distributor will provide a 20% cash deposit on signing the long form agreement. It is possible that the distributor will agree to pay installments of the agreed license fee based on set targets - such as start of production, end of principal, etc.

In the case of my film "Malaika" I had a significant pre-sale from Germany. My investor decided to put up a significant investment as equity based on this pre-sale – so it does work! Also we received a deposit!

Over my 15 years as an active sales agent I have had no distributor renege on a pre-sale contract – not even renegotiate, once the film was delivered. BUT, I have known of cases where distributors have received the completed film and just hated it – and cancelled the contract or re-negotiated the deal. Usually there is a good reason, such as the film package as presented to the distributor was not reflected in the film. For example, the part of the "named actor" was much longer in the script but was cut in the film for whatever reason. Often when a distributor makes a pre-buy based on an actor they will ensure that the actor has an agreed time on screen and a certain character in the script and that must be delivered on the screen. Naturally, should a distributor want to cancel a pre-buy on delivery then the producer must go to arbitration to force the distributor to pay – providing, of course, his contract has that clause. However, should the producer lose in arbitration and the distributor effectively cancels the deal then the producer has a completed film so the producer can and does have the ability to re-sell the film to another distributor and may end up re-selling the film for more than the pre-buy.

If a distributor does a pre-buy, a number of factors come into play. The distributor will have evaluated the film package very thoroughly to ensure it meets the needs of his requirements. Usually that distributor knows the sales agent and an element of trust from past film deals come into play. After all, the distributor is signing a binding contract on a film that is not made and that distributor is sending deposits and other installments to the sales agent/ producer without ever seeing the product. A true act of faith! I have seen many distributors lose their deposit from unscrupulous producers - so caveat emptor to all parties. With my film "Malaika" I had a pre-sale and received a deposit. My investor allowed the deposit to be used for production cash and he funded more money based on their pre-sale contract, but as I had a relationship with the foreign distributor he agreed to the fact we did not need a completion bond on the movie.

Many of the films I licensed in pre-sales were flat deals. That means one figure was agreed on as the license fee and that fee was usually fully paid on "accepted" delivery. Accepted means that all the terms and conditions of delivery were met. This one payment kept contracts and terms very simple and clean. Other contracts could include a license fee on delivery and then some form of profit split.

Two points here:

❖ Most of my films were low budget independent films and all parties wanted a clean, quick contract with no further activity required.

❖ I was always reluctant to enter into contracts that required the distributor to provide me accountings/royalty statements regularly. The ones I did get always showed the distributor not having to pay me any money based on their accounting. Did I want to spend thousands to go to Germany to audit them? I believed in the principal of "keep it simple stupid".

Certainly, I found during the 15 years of my sales agency, you build up relationships with the many buyers around the world and you are delivering product to them and they are paying you - that is the best business reference you can get. I sold hundreds of films for millions of dollars and I hardly remember one foreign sales contract going bad. However, that was more in the days of the heavy demand for video product and DVD product. Now the market is much more selective and much more careful what distributors want to buy to fill their pipeline.

Pre-sales are great instruments that can really help. Very often the case is that the pros outweigh the cons if you pre-sell a limited number of territories such as one or two of the major territories; and, of course, without pre-sales you might never even make the film.

Finally, a most important element concerns the need for a completion bond. When an entertainment bank accepts a distributor's contract as collateral and provides film financing they need to be sure the film will be finished and delivered per the contract to said distributor and that the distributor will then pay the bank off. To ensure the film is completed the film will have to contract a completion bond company (and pay for their services) and the bond company will ensure the film is completed. The bonding of a film is an area that requires considerable experience and knowledge to understand the many aspects of this important function.

PRE-SALE EXAMPLE

So let me provide you with an example of my own. In the late 90's, a writer/director submitted a family script to me entitled "Malaika" (see poster – four kids and an elephant!). I loved the script, the concept, the genre, so I, as a sales agent and film financier, agree to fund and distribute the film. The film's budget was under $1m. I was providing part of the budget from my own pocket but I also wanted to ensure that two or more of my international distributors liked the film project enough to pre-buy. I went to my favorite distributors in Germany and Japan. Both loved the project and committed. However, I found a private equity investor who acted as my banker for these pre-sales (so avoiding going to a bank and also avoiding a bond company involvement). The film got fully funded and was made and I sold it around the world. In the USA it was re-titled "Tons of Fun" so go buy it – it is a really fun family film!

FOREIGN TV REVENUE – DO NOT MISS OUT

In today's world of DIY distribution for indie filmmakers please take note of the following point. If we assume that 60-70% of all revenue for an independent feature film comes from foreign (and that is a reasonable empirical assumption) then we can assume that the foreign revenue comes from DVD sales/internet sales and also from TV. TV can play a large role in foreign revenue. If that is true, how does an independent filmmaker in the US tap into that revenue source? It seems that much of the talk at the AFM 2010 from independent filmmakers was about DIY distribution and online sales revenue with a large focus on domestic. This focus is fine. But, let us not forget where the majority of revenue comes from in the independent film business. Foreign DVD and TV are a very important part of that foreign revenue. A foreign sales agent has access to both DVD and TV buyers in all these foreign countries. USA based filmmakers usually do not. Therefore, to ignore sales agents can lead to an independent filmmaker missing out on a significant area of revenue - that being foreign TV sales.

PRODUCER – DIY WITH FOREIGN BUYERS

So now you know enough information to be dangerous to the film sales community. Just to help you a little more and if you are a filmmaker/producer who is planning to try and sell your film directly to a foreign buyer - here are a number of things you need to be aware of:

➢ The international film sales biz is highly complicated and changes constantly.
➢ Foreign buyers are always concerned with trust.
➢ Complete contracts and ensure product delivery requirements are met.
➢ Foreign buyers give priority to sales agents they know.
➢ Ensure the foreign buyer you are contacting handles your type of product.
➢ Unsolicited submissions from producers are not usually accepted. Contact them first and have them approve your submission – then send.

SALES AGENTS - TRICKS OF THE TRADE

❖ **Cross Collateralization** – Be careful if you see this term in a contract as it refers to offsetting financial losses in one market/media against the revenue of another or even another film you have with the agent.

❖ **Access to Film/Digital Masters** – NEVER, never, never allow the agent access to your film negative or digital masters. You provide to the agent such masters he wishes, based on licensing agreements for sales with buyers. However, I must warn you that the agent has ways around that control also. But, that is for another discussion...

❖ **Foreign Masters** – Sales agents deal with foreign buyers all the time and they maintain close relationship with them. It is not out of the realm of reality that should an agent want to obtain a foreign master directly from a foreign buyer they can do that.

❖ **Sequels** – Ensure you are aware that the agreement you sign with a sales agent has the correct wording you wish regarding sequel rights.

❖ **Splitting Revenue on Titles/Territories** – This is a difficult one for a producer to even be aware of, as it usually happens behind closed doors. It refers to the value an agent places on a film when your film is sold as part of a larger package. It may be that an agent gets a bigger commission from films other than your film - so in a package deal the agent may allot more revenue to the higher commission films than yours. Hopefully, you have minimums in place to help mitigate such actions.

❖ **Term – But Longer Really!** – You, as the producer, have set a time limit on the agreement with the sales agent. That agreement is about to expire so you go to hire another agent. Be aware that the old agent may have sold territories for terms years longer than his contract with you. Those contracts must be honored and the agent must receive his commission on those sales.

❖ **Airlines** – This is often a source of income that is forgotten by producers. If the film is suitable for airlines to show to their passengers (family is always good) then you can sell to many airlines all over the world and make good sales.

❖ **Marketing Materials** - Now here is a concern for a producer! Often filmmakers have little money left for marketing after the completion of the film, but a film agent can, and does, put up the money for trailers, artwork, posters, etc. Naturally, the agent will charge a premium for such services and also get his money back from first monies received from any licensing deals. Producers must understand that and negotiate reasonable prices for such materials up front. I have seen plenty of producers get stung by exorbitant prices for marketing materials even when done by third parties because agents do deals with those third parties.

This brings me to another dangerous area for producers! The fact that the sales agents do deals with third parties on all sorts of matters to do with selling a producer's film is a real control problem for producers who actually would like to see money back from licensing deals. What do I mean with that comment? Sales agents use the same creative companies to help them with trailers, artwork/posters, etc. So they arrange a cost structure from those vendors that create fees back to the agent based on full price invoices to producers. Often in contracts between producer and sales agent the producer tries to protect himself with paying only third party invoices for work done on his film marketing material say, but the third party has an arrangement with the agent for a discount due to their relationship. Now you producers take this one step further and imagine a similar arrangement on delivery items that can be very expensive and take it even further when you look at licensing deals made by the agent with foreign distributors and the actual price written on the contract for your film. Is that really the price for licensing your film or an arranged price that hides a higher price – the difference goes where?

There are so many areas that producers face in finalizing an agreement with a sales agent that I can go on and on; but, I hope these points can be of assistance to you. It is best to get a recommendation from an industry insider who knows sales agents and secondly, get a lawyer to help you.

REALITY CHECK FOR FILMMAKERS – THE TRUTH & NOTHING BUT THE TRUTH!

The following comments need to be stated to assist filmmakers understand what this independent film sales business is all about. Let us dismiss some of the myths about what your film is worth and what it means to sell your film.

❖ No one cares how much time and sweat you have put into the making of your film.

❖ No one cares how many dollars you have spent on your film. The film stands alone on what is on the screen – whether you spent $10 or $10m a buyer will look at it in terms of how much he can make for the film in his territory.

❖ The commerciality of any genre at any given time is dependent on the demands of the marketplace at the time of sale. One genre can be hot for a time then drop off suddenly with prices following.

❖ One major misconception with filmmakers is that there are set prices for film licensing based on budget and genre, etc. for each territory. – NO! There is no one figure buyers will pay for any film – period. There is a range of prices buyers might pay (based on such variables as commerciality, budget, stars, etc.) but not one set price.

❖ Sales estimates or sales projections are just that – estimates! There are no prices carved in stone in the film business.

❖ All rights? All rights usually mean all the film rights – namely theatrical, DVD, television, and internet, plus ancillary markets.

❖ Because a distributor acquires all rights from a filmmaker/producer does not mean he will or can exploit all rights. It does not mean the distributor will provide a theatrical release or get a major TV deal – no! It means that they are the sole licensor to your film for those rights acquired and it is their decision which rights, when and how they will exploit those rights.

❖ Territory and those rights - usually with intellectual property the territory is one of the important contractual elements and with film it is not unusual to split territories into various option packages - namely worldwide rights or domestic rights (USA/Canada) and/or foreign rights. Therefore, it is also not unusual to have a distributor in the US acquire all rights for domestic (USA/Canada) and a foreign sales agent acquire all rights for foreign. The sales agent will then sell the film territory by territory and may split rights within territories - eg. Sell DVD rights to one company and TV rights to a TV channel, both in the same territory.

❖ The budget of your film may or may not have a bearing on the price paid by a buyer. The buyer is looking for many factors in his decision including cast, genre, production quality, story, acting, slot, etc. If one or more of those elements are not in the film, then the price may be much lower or no offer at all. That is reality!

❖ What is your budget? That by itself is a great question. Is it only a cash budget? Is it a budget that includes all your actor, director, producer deferrals? Does the budget include the fact you got a package deal on your camera and lighting equipment for net profit points. Does it include all the soft money you received that you do not have to pay back? Does it include benefits in kind like cars for advertising? What really is your budget? Oh yes — most film professionals especially buyers, can see what the budget should be by what is on the screen so they tend to dismiss producer budget figures.

WHAT IS A PRODUCER'S REP - CAN THEY HELP?

One can define a producer's rep as an adviser/consultant to filmmakers. They can be contracted to advise a producer/filmmaker at all phases of the production, financing, marketing or distribution of a film project. Usually the rep helps in establishing connections that will benefit the producer in the film project's journey to the final consumer.

Often the best reps are instrumental in assisting filmmakers obtain the best sales agent and/or distributor for their film project and even assist in film financing. Many such reps are lawyers with their own entertainment law practices so they have their fingers on the pulse of the film business. Naturally, for their services they charge a fee that can range from 5% upwards, of the financing or revenue generated from the project or a monthly retainer or even a fee structure to be negotiated depending on circumstances.

Can they help you? Yes, but...They are advisors and you still need to sign on a sales agent or distributor and they all take fees too. I would suggest that if you are blissfully ignorant of the film business, especially how it works in Los Angeles, then consider obtaining the services of a rep. If you feel comfortable with doing your own research and investigation of agents and distributors then no do not hire a rep.

WHAT IS A BUYER'S REP - ARE THEY RELEVANT TO YOU?

Usually they are based in Los Angeles and they represent international buyers. They provide data, research, support and expertise to international film buyers. They work with each of their buyer clients to develop and implement a customized strategy to ensure that each is meeting their acquisitions goals, whether clients are focused on the top theatrical films in the marketplace, a steady pipeline of TV/DVD titles, or festival and specialized releases.

Specific activities of a buyer's rep are:

➢ Product updates on new titles announced by sales companies and other sources.
➢ Script coverage and screening reports.
➢ Introductions to independent and studio sources for product.
➢ Pre-film market availability report for each client territory.
➢ Assistance with markets: scheduling appointments, registration, screening schedule.
➢ Assistance in negotiation and follow-up with contracts and servicing
➢ Between markets, acquisitions follow up.

There are a select number of these buyer's representatives. They often represent the bigger buyers in each of the major territories; therefore, they are good people to know as they are always looking out for good commercial film projects and can provide pre-sale financing as well as licensing your completed film.

FILM MARKETS

WHAT IS THE DIFFERENCE BETWEEN A FILM MARKET AND A FILM FESTIVAL?

❖ *Film Market:* Venue organized for commercial reasons, not for general public. Content providers and buyers from theatrical, TV and DVD buyers from all over the world meet to license product.

❖ *Film Festival:* Venue organized around film screenings and prizes, dedicated to introduce movies of a certain style to a paying public audience attended by opinion makers and journalists seeking stories, acquisition executives looking for product for distribution and, of course, the filmmakers themselves to gain the film business attention by being see on the big screen, by winning prizes and by having their film product gain publicity and public acclaim.

FILM MARKETS/FESTIVALS

- American Film Market (AFM) - (Los Angeles/Oct-Nov)
- Cannes Film Festival/Market - (France/ May)
- European Film Market/Berlin Film Festival - (Berlin/February)
- MIPCOM - (France/Oct) - TV/Video
- MIPTV - (Cannes France/April) - TV product
- NAPTE - (US/January) - Film/TV product
- Sundance Film Festival - (US/January)
- Toronto Film Festival - (Toronto/September)
- LA Screenings - (Los Angeles/June) - TV product

THE AMERICAN FILM MARKET/AFM

This is the premiere global marketplace for motion picture production and distribution and the largest gathering of film industry professionals in North America.

The AFM is the largest motion picture trade show in the world and a pivotal destination for independent filmmakers and industry executives. A unique marketplace to develop, package, pitch, finance, license and distribute film product. Over 8,000 attendees from around the world attend AFM for eight days in the fall each year:

2010: November 3 – 10

- 2011: November 2 – 9
- 2012: October 31 - November 7

The business of independent motion picture production and distribution, a truly collaborative process, reaches its peak every year at the American Film Market. For eight days there is deal-making, screenings, seminars, red carpet premieres, networking and parties. Participants come from all over the world and include acquisition and development executives, agents, attorneys, directors, distributors, festival directors, financiers, film commissioners, producers, writers, the world's press, all those who provide services to the motion picture industry.

Why is the AFM so prestigious?

1) More than 1,500 buyers attend
2) 70+ countries represented
3) 400+ sales companies and production entities attend
4) Sellers see more buyers at AFM than at Cannes
5) The AFM is housed under one roof. – Lowes Hotel, Santa Monica
6) Excellent facilities for both buyers and sellers
7) The AFM is six months after Cannes so buyers will be open to license again
8) LA is the film industry capital
9) 500 film screenings are shown
10) 100 film premiers
11) Over 1000 new films/projects presented

The Loews Santa Monica Beach Hotel and the Le Merigot Beach Hotel are converted into a busy film marketplace. All 23 screens on the Santa Monica Promenade (3rd street) and the surrounding community become AFM screening rooms for the entire eight-day event and eight digital and video screening rooms are added just for the AFM. 2009 was my 18th AFM.

The American Film Market is produced by the Independent Film & Television Alliance (www.ifta-online.org). Every industry has "majors" and "independents". The same is true in the entertainment industry. An independent film or TV program is financed primarily from sources outside the six major US studios. Independent product is made at every budget range and is seen side-by-side with major studio releases. As the voice and advocate for independents worldwide, IFTA speaks out on critical matters, including the threat to a competitive marketplace posed by media consolidation and net neutrality, and the need to foster broad-based growth of the industry. IFTA Members are companies that are active in production, licensing and financing of programming for international distribution.

The AFM has strict access rules and is not for the general public. It is a professional film executive trade show for those who are involved in licensing theatrical, DVD, TV rights, etc. The AFM does allow the purchase of a "badge" or pass that will allow full access to the market for those who are not fully accredited buyers or sellers - so an independent filmmaker can get into the market to sell or pitch their product.

THE MARCHE DU FILM (www.marchedufilm.com)
To serve and promote the dual nature of film, as both a cultural and economic enterprise, the Festival de Cannes created the Film Market in 1959, so as to lend some of its own energy to the international film industry.

In 2009, Cannes received film professionals the world over, welcoming 10,000 participants from 101 countries representing 4,000 companies, with 400 exhibitors. Producers, sellers, distributors and financiers came to do business.

Each year the film market encourages the film industry to do business by giving the industry a place to meet and by providing professionals (and the Producer's Network) with services and tools to facilitate their meeting, discussions and film negotiations. Last year approx. 4,000 films and projects were presented; 1,500 screenings took place, 75% of which were premieres.

TO CANNES OR NOT TO CANNES!
Should producers/filmmakers try to sell their film(s) at a film market?
This discussion really concerns two film markets - one is Cannes and the second is the American Film Market. These markets are the premiere markets for licensing independent films and, in my opinion, are the most fun and the most informative. However, the question a producer/filmmaker needs to ask is - what is the purpose of going to

such a market and in what manner do you wish to participate at the market? So let us look at those options.

To go just as an observer and see what is happening is one course of action. Certainly, the AFM as it is based in LA and many filmmakers are also based in LA provides an excellent opportunity to see how films are sold and bought. However, you need to get a "pass" to allow yourself on to the main hotel floors where the sales offices are. Go to the AFM website for costs of day passes or try to get a pass from one of the sales companies who have an AFM office, as they have guest passes. At the AFM it is on the upper floors of the Loews Hotel where the sales activity occurs. Many producers also hang out around the pool and in the bar/ lobby area of the hotel as many buyers/sellers meet in this area to socialize with sellers, buyers, actors, directors and other filmmakers. In fact, a producer approached me with a trailer of his film in the lobby. He showed his trailer to me then and there and I ended up liking it and during the AFM I signed a deal with him. I started selling his film at that market. So opportunity does come knocking and things do happen!

Attending a film market will certainly provide you an opportunity to feel and hear what the sales business is about. Pay attention to your surroundings and look at the films being sold, trailers being shown. Look at the trade papers "bumper" market issues that list many of the sales companies attending the market and the type of products they are selling and what is selling. A market is a great place to do research on different sales agency companies and how they present their films and what types of films they represent. Remember a film market is where independent films get sold and bought – the money is here – so markets are very important.

A second and more involved course of action is to sell your own film(s) at a market and becoming an exhibitor. This would involve you getting a booth/sales office at the AFM and setting up that office in the Lowes hotel to sell your product. There are variations on this option. I will concentrate on just one and that involves setting up your own mini sales company and hiring a sales person to assist you in the selling/ licensing of your films. The following are the processes the filmmaker/ producer need to address to follow this option:

➢ Usually, a producer has more than just one completed film to sell.

➢ Usually this option will cover, at a minimum, AFM and Cannes.
➢ This option requires the hiring, for a period of time, an experienced sales person, especially in the foreign territory area to prepare for the markets, sell at the markets, and follow up on sales contracts/ delivery after the markets.
➢ The sales person will have access to the worldwide network of buyers contact information. That person will inform the buyers of product and set up meetings at the market with buyers.
➢ The producer will pay all the costs of the AFM booth and becoming an exhibitor at the market, marketing material, equipment, etc.

This option then allows the producer to control all facets of the sales and marketing operation and reap the rewards of gross sales without the middle man sales agent costs and dilution of control. I have seen this type of operation be successful and it can develop into a viable going concern to sell films and nurture new projects. It is very beneficial for sales companies to build up a reputation with foreign buyers and to build working relationships that benefit all parties. To be an exhibitor means you are serious about selling films.

An important factor in deciding which option is viable is the cost involved. Certainly, when you look at the costs of the AFM compared to Cannes there are significant differences. With both markets one has to purchase a market pass and if you are to be an exhibitor then cost of a booth/sales office package will be necessary. Those exhibitor costs are many thousands of dollars. Go to the AFM website and/or the Marche Du Film site for costs of a market pass and the cost of exhibitor's package. Each market has their own variations on market passes so chose the pass that best suites you.

Being an exhibitor has many benefits. An important one is that you receive a full and complete list of all the buyers attending the market with contact information. In the options we discussed, a producer just going to a market to explore will not have access to the buyer lists; but, with the exhibitor option the person who is the sales person will have this list already, as they will need such a list before hand to set up meetings with buyers in the preparation stage.

Another benefit of being an exhibitor is that you can have a market screening for buyers and be listed in the market screening guide.

Producer note – always try to ensure your booth/sales office at the market is in a prime location. Often location is determined by price and your longevity at attending the market. For newbies, try your best to get the best location and that means knowing the physical layout of the hotel/center and knowing best traffic areas.

The exhibitor option I have seen work and work well, but it takes a producer/filmmaker to front considerable costs and also the sales company formed needs product – ie. more than just one film. The AFM is in Los Angeles and Cannes is in the south of France. Huge costs arise with the Cannes market - flights, hotels and shipping costs. Those costs can be and usually are major factors that require attention and consideration.

Both the AFM and Cannes last for 10 days. The first halves of the markets are usually busy with selling and buying activity. During the second half of the market the pace drops and other film matters come into play. This includes new projects, co-productions, financing options, development deals, etc.

Remember, if you sign up with a sales agent they front those market/ marketing costs for you and recoup them from sales. A sales agent knows the market and how to conduct business. You as a producer lose a degree of control and you have to pay commission on sales. Which way to go is a dilemma that only you can make based on your own circumstances and the information available to you.

Finally, it is paramount that before you attend your film market you have extensive knowledge on selling your film. This will include territory pricing, negotiating knowledge and an ability to talk the film sales language needed in such a professional arena. Film professionals hate to have to talk with filmmakers/producers who really do not understand the film biz and especially not the selling of films to foreign territories.

CANNES FILM MARKET 2010, 2000, 1990 – RETROSPECTIVE

The Cannes Film Festival – a most excellent event! The Oscars and the Cannes Film Festival are the two most glamorous, prestigious and fun events in the film industry calendar.

Cannes 2010 was my 18th Cannes Film Festival - or should I say 18th March du Film, as I really never go to the festival part of Cannes, but to the Marche which is the film market side. The Marche is a major meeting place for film professionals. Each year buyers, distributors and producers converge on Cannes for ten days of meetings and negotiations in a film market setting just behind the main Palais de festival. This unique international event allows all professionals to develop their projects, present their latest films for sale, establish partnerships and co-productions and meet old friends. As I said, 2010 was my 18th Cannes Film Festival, going back to 1986, although I have been to Cannes many more times attending MIPCOM, which is essentially a TV, DVD product driven market for buying, selling, financing and distributing entertainment content.

Many producers and filmmakers ask me how productive is it to attend a film market for a non–professional film sales person. My answer to that is not productive at all unless...Unless you come fully prepared and well organized. That means knowing what goes on in these markets and understanding the process. If you do that, then an AFM or a Cannes can be very positive.

It is important to understand that, for film professionals that are selling/buying product, Cannes and AFM are film markets not festivals. The markets are not to show off your film and get prizes and applause from the general public. A film market is a commercial concern, not for the general public. – This is business! – The business of licensing films to worldwide buyers for theatrical, DVD and television rights and also for developing new products.

Over the many years I have been a sales agent, I have made a great many friends around the world that I see at the film markets and often only see them at the markets; although we constantly correspond, exchanging information on which films are available for their territories. It is amazing that I have known so many buyers for over twenty years and they are very much old friends.

I want to discuss with you how you as an independent filmmaker or producer can benefit by attending these industry markets in my next blog - but first I want to discuss with you the Cannes market I see today compared to markets 10 years ago and even earlier – it is extraordinary how similar they are – yet so different!

❖ **Cannes - "The Golden Age" - 1990**

This was the boom years for the independent film industry with money flowing to make product and that product was in high demand all over the world. In those days you could make virtually anything (and we tried believe me! - all sorts of rubbish pictures flowed out of independent Hollywood) and it would sell, especially horror, action and those sexy thrillers. There was a huge number of action stars - from Dolph Lundgren to Sly and Van Dam.

I received money to make films based on a one page synopsis and great art work! I could sell them all over the world without much trouble – those were the days! Money flowed from equity players, corporate players, soft money from governments and, of course, pre-sales.

❖ **Cannes - "Times they had changed!" - 2000**

Times definitely had changed! – The video boom had past and revenue had dropped significantly for independent films. DVD was new, VHS was old hat, but income was much lower. This meant selling films was harder and buyers would cherry pick films that had specific places in their release schedules or TV slots. Gone was the boom. Producers and filmmakers had to really be aware of what buyers wanted and at what price they were prepared to pay for the product.

Film packaging (script, genre, budget, cast, director) became a clear and obvious necessity. It was tempered by knowledge and understanding of what sells in the US, but also in foreign, as foreign accounted for the majority of income and that was mainly in the DVD and television sectors. The era of full availability of pre-sales from many of the major territories had, in many instances, dried up. An independent film package now had to be exceptional with very commercial elements to attract and receive significant pre-sales to assist in funding. This we find even more through the 2000's up until now.

Where has the money come from?

It is interesting to look at the different financing options that have become available to the independent film industry over these many years since I entered it in 1987. In the late 1980s, companies like Carolco, Live Home Video and Canon were very active and were very prominent publically traded independent film companies as the video boom for product was expanding all over the world. Product such as Terminator, Rambo and Basic Instinct created large audiences around the world but soon that bubble burst and those companies went bankrupt or insolvent.

Round about that time the international bank, Credit Lyonnais, and a number of other European banks entered the independent film industry to help fund the purchase of MGM. Unfortunately for all, that investment went like much investment in the film business – down the toilet!

The Europeans kept their fingers in the investment pie, but then came the Japanese with investments into Universal and Sony. Again large losses were incurred. But, it must be said, through the early 1990's pre-sales were still present and active.

It is always amazing how this industry every few years comes up with another innovative financing approach. Certainly a major player for a time was the insurance-backed financing. These insurance companies entered the film business and basically approached it as an insurance business strategy covering various financing strategies. They received large premiums; but, unfortunately, many of the multi-film packages they covered went bad and lawsuits flourished. The 2001 Artisan Insurance backed lawsuit regarding a three year deal to guarantee some $500m in bank loans was a memorable one. There were many other lawsuits with many players.

Another of these innovative financing ventures came directly from Germany and the new trading market available to independent film companies. These ventures provided companies like Helkon, VCL and Senator new funds to invest heavily into US films. Once again the story of losses dominated the trade papers. The Germans however, did not give up. They moved forward and presented the tax-shelter financings that once again provided Hollywood with substantial funds - until a point came where the German tax authorities called "enough"!

Soft Money – Of course, over the many years since I entered the sales agency side of the biz, many foreign countries have and still do offer soft money film financing avenues. Such soft money as various tax incentives, rebates and grants are an important source of production financing for films shooting in Canada, Australia, UK, etc. In the last few years the USA has stepped forward with their own soft money options with many states providing their own variations to encourage films to shoot in their state. Such soft money options can contribute up to and more than 25% of a production budget; but, be aware that these soft money options come with strict rules and conditions of entitlement.

Even today new financing schemes pop up. For example, the US private-equity funds. I am confident new schemes will arise at regular intervals into the future. The world of the independent film company is a precarious one. The biggest obstacle being that they do not have guaranteed distribution. Secondly, they do not have the very deep pockets of the major studios who can weather the storms of multiple film failures. Studios know that over time they will get a hit or two and then a big blockbuster that will pay for all the failures.

❖ Cannes - "What now?" - 2010 and onwards

Certainly it is true in 2010 it is the easiest time in history to make a film, but it is also the hardest time to sell it. Digital technology has enabled filmmakers to shoot films easily and cheaply, but to sell – oh to sell! The difficulty is selling and if you can sell, at what price? The amount of research into the type of film you wish to make and its constituent elements has to be substantial if you have any hope of commercial success. It is obvious that many filmmakers make films without any due regard to its commercial success. The creative flair is good to possess as a writer/producer. But, if you wish to sell the film you need to make sure you understand the demands, needs and requirement of who will buy your film.

Remember, you've spent time – you've spent money to make your film. How much is that film worth? NOTHING... until someone buys it.

Also, do not forget one of the most important aspects of Cannes – the parties – oh yes the parties! I would have to get into training to be able to take the hours and hours of late night partying. One of the best independent parties ever thrown at the Cannes film market was produced by a company I was a principal of namely, Capital Entertainment, out of Zurich Switzerland. This great party that lives in folklore at Cannes was the "Too Hot to Trotsky Party". There was in later years a "Too Hot to Trotsky II Party" but it wasn't as big a success as the original. How often does that happen in the film business!!

DIY: CANNES TIMELINE/SCHEDULE OF ACTIVITIES

To assist those producers/filmmakers who plan to go to either Cannes and/or the AFM and wish to become an exhibitor and sell their own films at a major film market the following is a timeline/schedule of activities I have compiled based on my own schedule as a sales agent going to Cannes:

❑ **Three months prior to Cannes:**
- Acquire product or produce your own
- Begin preparation of:
  Artwork/Image/Tagline/Text/Photos
  Trailers/35mm prints, etc.
- Book market office and company details in Marche directory
- Book flights/hotels

❑ **Two months prior to Cannes:**
- Finalize film product line up
- Updates on artwork, trailers & marketing materials
- Prepare trailers and prepare film advertisements for trade mags
- Send list of films selling and market office location to the trade papers, ie. Hollywood Reporter/Variety/Screen Int., etc.
- Lock in screenings times/locations at market

❑ **One month prior to Cannes:**
- For the product line up:
  Finalize artwork
  Finalize trailers
  Finalize all agreements for film product
- Order large posters
- Order all market office equipment
- Prepare product reel
- Prepare film DVDs to be duplicated
- Email 100 countries/1000+ buyers' product line up
- Email buyers potential meeting times
- Order 500 one sheets/flyers of each film represented
- Order 200 DVDs of product reel
- Order 50 DVDs of each film represented

- Place all film advertisements in trade papers
- ☐ **Arrival at Cannes/the Market:**
  - Market/Marche Du Film – accreditation
  - Set up market office
  - Set up display posters, trailers, screeners, reel, etc.
  - Prepare drinks, food and schedule for 10 days
  - Have over 100 meetings with buyers - 50 countries
  - Attend screenings of your films
  - Ensure you attend the Playboy party!!

FILM FESTIVALS

Film Festival: Venue organized around film screenings and prizes, dedicated to introduce movies of a certain style to a paying public audience attended by opinion makers and journalists seeking stories; also attended by acquisition executives looking for product for distribution and, of course, by the filmmakers themselves to gain the film business attention by having their film seen on the big screen, by winning prizes and having their film product gain publicity and public acclaim.

A film festival can do good things for your film and for a filmmaker's development. Having your independent film screened at one of the several hundred festivals in the USA can do three things for you:

1) Attract an audience for your film
2) Provide a film industry marketplace for you
3) Provide an environment to help you learn about the film biz

The film festival world has greatly changed since I first submitted a film to Geoff Gilmore at a small festival back in 1990 called Sundance Film Festival. The film was "The Cabinet of Dr. Ramirez" – a remake of the famous Cabinet of Dr. Calgari. Back then a few festivals existed but with the dramatic rise of independent film production in the 1990's, festivals multiplied to where there are over 650 in the US now and growing.

Like everything in business you should know what you want to achieve by entering your film in a festival. Which festival? Is it to get a sales agent? Do you just wish for accolades? Do you want to sell your film to a distributor?

Many festivals no longer accept direct submissions. They direct you to an online festival submission service (eg. www.withoutabox.com). This process helps navigate filmmakers through the process of festival selection and submission for US and international festivals. Festivals are great places to meet like-minded people who are genuinely interested in film. Often great contacts can be made in all aspects of the film industry. Often such festivals are attended by film acquisition executives from all levels of film companies – from majors to little sales companies.

Festivals make a great deal of effort to ensure they have their own unique DNA/brand. Certain festivals have gained well deserved reputations as being a place to discover film gems that have gone into distribution and made $$$. Notable examples are:

- Sex Lies and Videotape: Cost $1.2m / US BO $24.7m
- Blair Witch: Cost $60k / World BO $ 249m

A film that is well written, has a good story, is well acted, has good production value, good visuals, and good sound track and is entertaining will do well at a festival and/or in distribution. – Correct?

Here are some pointers to help your future film do well at a film festival:

➢ Make sure the script you shot is professional and structured.
➢ Tell a story not just a vignette.
➢ Do not over embellish your film with fat.
➢ Get real actors – please!
➢ Use post-production well to enhance your film.
➢ Sound – make sure your sound is good.
➢ Try to entertain – your day to day life on film is often boring!

Here are some film festival big mistakes by filmmakers when trying to submit a film for entry:

➢ Sending a rough cut of the film. Wait until you are done with the film and happy. Never send a rough cut.
➢ Submitting the film to every festival possible all at once – NO! Choose which festivals carefully based on your requirements and best fit. Often the better festivals insist on a "premier" status of a film - that means they are exclusive to show it if accepted.

> Sending marketing materials. Just send the film. Sending press kits and posters, etc. do not help. Just submit the film and what the festival asks for.
> Do not call/harass festival staff – NO!
> Have a plan – place festivals in an order and carry it out.

HOW DOES ATTENDING A FILM FESTIVAL BENEFIT FILMMAKERS/PRODUCERS?

Film festivals, especially the more important ones (Cannes/Sundance/Toronto/Berlin/Tribeca), have become lucrative hunting grounds for acquisition executives from all levels of the film industry, both domestic and internationally. They want to find that gem that they can acquire for a small amount of money and through their distribution chain make buckets of money from! However, those gems are very hard to find.

Film festivals can also be lucrative for filmmakers and producers who do not have a film screening, who wish to exploit the availability of opportunities that avail them at festivals, as acquisition executives and buyers are all in the festival location. Benefits can include:

> Attend seminars, panels and, of course, parties for networking purposes.
> Try to get buyers/acquisition execs to take meetings on your projects.
> Attend film screenings. This will provide ideas for what is being produced. Hopefully you will see what is being bought and what audiences like.
> Make sure you collect business cards of those attending and any magazines about the film business. (Ensure your business card is professional and presents contact information.)
> Take note – you never know who you may meet at a festival - could be a studio head or just a newbie. Always be professional. Usually after a short conversation you will know how knowledgeable the person is. From that you can evaluate their potential contribution to your advancement.
> Network with other filmmakers and acquire practical experiences that may benefit you.

Besides the top level of film festivals there are also a number of second level festivals. These include Telluride FF/Los Angeles FF/AFI/ Slamdance/Raindance/Hamptons/Palm Springs FF - I have attended many of these festivals and have had great fun and met many really beneficial filmmakers and producers.

10 THINGS YOU SHOULD KNOW ABOUT SELLING YOUR OWN FILM

1) **Understand the Film Business** - Please ensure you study and search out information about selling/marketing independent films. Find out what are the important areas to look for and the pitfalls to avoid. Research the different revenue streams, their value and the order of maximizing your revenue. Take time and effort to learn the business. Understand the terms and phraseology of the film industry. There is nothing more frustrating to a film professional than dealing with an amateur who lacks rudimentary understanding of the business of film.

2) **Don't Believe Your Own Hype** - Keep realistic and down to earth. I have seen so many times filmmakers believe their film is so great it has to go theatrical and will make millions....and are shocked no one wants to even buy it! Always try to keep a realistic expectation of potential revenues and check out revenues of similar type films – genre, actors, budget level, etc.

3) **Film Ready?** - As a filmmaker, make sure your film is in the best shape you can make it before you bring it to festivals or to acquisition people. I also know that you can keep trying to enhance your film and overdo it. One producer I know of kept re-editing and changing it with months passing and he missed AFM!

4) **Prepare a Marketing/Sales Strategy and Stick With It** - Decide if a festival route is best or whether you should contact DVD distributors direct or whether to go yourself to the AFM or even Cannes or go the internet route or even four wall! Ensure that you control and monitor where and to whom you distribute screenings of your film.

5) **Timing** - If you are selling your own film it is so important to check on dates of festivals and markets so you can plan ahead.

6) **Who's Who** - Research and do your homework on which sales/ distribution companies, festivals and markets are best for your film. Prepare a database of key executives you need to contact. That needs to be current as executives move around companies a lot.

7) **What Is Your Film Worth?** - Nothing unless someone buys it! So ensure your marketing materials are good and hopefully you have a good story, well-acted, well shot, etc.

8) **Rep or No Rep?** - Sometimes you as the filmmaker are not fully equipped to sell the film or even find the right sales agent/ distributor and that is where a good producer rep can help you. Consider all angles with this approach then move one way or another.

9) **Outside Opinions** - This can be a double edged sword. This is your film, your creation and an outsider may or may not like your vision. It helps to get an opinion from someone who knows the market/ sales of your genre of film. They can give you an appraisal on its sales value. I also had a producer who showed the film to many people until he got a positive from one of them and as he got the validation he was looking for he stopped. The film was bad and he did not want to listen. Again, the value is in who pays what for it and that depends on many factors including timing and getting to the right buyers.

10) **Deal Closing** - I have dealt with producers that have an inflated view of the value of a film. An offer comes in for a certain territory and they feel it is low. They disregard the opinion of the sales agent and they prefer to wait. If the sales agent advises to take then take. Should you not take the offer and the film does not sell during the market it then becomes a product at the next market that has already been shopped in a previous market. Buyers always seem to be attracted to new product, fresh at a market. Not always the case, but one in the hand is worth two in the bush! It is so important to review your sales status as films sell piece meal, ie. – usually territory by territory. You need to evaluate sales estimates to actuals and what territories are sold or not sold. Here your sales agent has to provide his experience and knowledge.

FILM FINANCING

HIGHLIGHTS OF THIS CHAPTER...

SOURCES OF FILM FINANCING

INVESTORS!

THE BUSINESS PLAN

SOFT MONEY — USA & FOREIGN

18 THINGS YOU SHOULD KNOW
ABOUT FILM FINANCING

FILM FINANCING
"Show Me The Money"

HOW IT REALLY IS!
How do you make a small fortune in the film business?
Start off with a big one!!!! How true is that?

Let us talk some truths about film financing. Firstly, there are always many different ways to finance a feature film. Often it is a combination of options that can work the best. Secondly, there are always negatives and positives to any form of financing you decide on to fund a film. So, there is a need to evaluate options to maximize your success. Thirdly, there are no rules. If all the parties agree on whatever formula you have put together and it works, then great. However, do not be under any illusion that financing a film is easy. It most definitely is not and the old line about a film is never financed unless you are actually spending the money is true. Even then – do you have you enough for post?

The economic downturn from 2008/9/10 onwards has created a scarcity of funding from traditional funding sources such as equity, loans and pre-sales. Consumers for film/TV product have had shifting patterns, especially involving online consumption of content and the consumer's expectation that content should be free. This has negatively affected the upside of revenue for films. Technology has helped lower the costs of producing independent films and has also provided amazing access to new distribution channels. Therefore, we find a major increase in film projects chasing a smaller amount of funding. Naturally, innovative film financing avenues have to be explored to help fill the gap. These avenues include soft money (tax incentives), deferral agreements with talent/crew/suppliers, product placement, plus internet funding, which includes crowd funding.

Funding depends on the film vehicle you are attempting to finance. In the case of this discussion we will focus on the independent feature film. Financing usually refers to production financing, the actual funds necessary to make the film; however, financing can and often does include development financing as well as marketing/P&A financing.

For our discussion we will not focus on studio financing other than a short description on how studios fund their films and the negative pick-up option. The world of studio film financing is usually not relevant to the world of independent feature films. In fact, The Independent Film and Television Alliance (formerly known as AFMA) stipulates that a film is classed as an independent film if "more than 50% of its financing comes from sources other than major studios". Such a statement covers a wide range of film types, budget levels and genres. One would question the above definition by the IFTA as it is my experience that should a studio fund up to 50% of a production budget that film will most likely be released in the USA by a major studio thereby making it a studio picture. We can discuss this matter at length, but, for the purposes of this discussion the independent film is financed by an independent producer who has raised the majority of funds outside the studio system.

FILM FINANCING EXAMPLE:
An example of funding an independent feature film can come from of a number of different sources.
1) Producer covers development money for the script and limited marketing materials.
2) Sales agent provides three major territories pre-sales covering 40% of the production budget.
3) Producer makes a post-production deal for costs of all post-production/editing/sound/optical including delivery masters. Deal includes high position in order of recoupment for agreed costs and % of net profits.
4) Producer presents all of the above to an equity investor who agrees to fund the balance of the production budget, plus finance the pre-sale contracts so that no bank is required and no completion bond is required.
5) Film is now ready to go into production.
    Does this seem feasible? Look at the different financing options utilized by the producer to make the whole transaction work. This is not just a theoretical example but a real life example of a film financing package that worked. It worked for me, I got it produced and distributed around the world. The budget was around $1m. It is

certainly a rare occurrence to have a private investor hand you a check for a large sum right up front and off you go into production fully funded! That has happened to me and it is truly a wondrous event. Of course, when you have a rich investor who does this type of thing be prepared to have him very involved in the film especially in the matter of getting his investment back!

Film financing by definition requires the ability to blend the world of film with the world of finance and also blend the world of commerce with the world of creativity. This is indeed a daunting task! The creative brain butts heads with the financially pragmatic investor. As a general rule the two components of film financing revolve around control and budget.

LOSE CONTROL!

The bigger the budget the less autonomy a producer/filmmaker has because other players become involved and that limits total freedom to act as you may wish. As a budget gets larger it moves from a self-financing model to a hybrid independent financing model. And, as the budget gets really large it moves into a studio type financing model. At each stage the filmmaker/producer will lose a certain degree of autonomy to control where and how the film project is to manifest itself.

THE BUDGET

Often it is assumed that all low budget films are independent because all large budget films are studio pictures. Generally that is an accurate statement. Certainly for the purposes of our discussion independent film financing concerns low budget films – so what are the budgets we are really talking about. I will suggest that independent film budgets fall into four categories:

- *Micro Budget:*   *$100k or less*
- *Ultra-Low Budget:*   *$1m Or less*
- *Low Budget:*   *$2.5m or less*
- *Low-Mid Budget:*   *$10m and under*

Budgets in excess of $10m are almost always deemed to be beyond the independent realm, although not always!

SO YOU HAVE A SCRIPT – WHAT NOW IN TERMS OF FINANCING?

Film financing is a complex and daunting task to any new filmmaker. Over my many years in the biz it is a usual scenario for me to be approached by a budding "Spielberg" filmmaker who has all the enthusiasm and creative flair but has no real idea how to get his recently completed screenplay financed. As you will see there are many film financing options. How they can fit together is also a process. So let us look at the process a newbie filmmaker should look to in order to get started.

Firstly, a good question is "what amount of film financing are you looking for?" This is a really loaded question as often the filmmaker has no real idea. I want $50m and I want Brad Pitt to be the lead is not a realistic option - but I've heard it before! We need to look at the script, its genre, its locations and settings to gain an idea if a budget is realistic. An important part of that evaluation is the level of actors the filmmaker feels appropriate for the script. Often newbie filmmakers have incredibly high expectations on the level of actors a new filmmaker can get for their script. It is highly unlikely an A or A- actor will even be interested in this script so go for a more reasonable B type actor as part of your wish list and then budget accordingly. It is important to have a budget that is reasonable and potentially attainable. Remember any investor will look at who the filmmaker is and what they bring to the table. Certainly, if the filmmaker is a complete novice and has little understanding of the film business it would seem reasonable for the filmmaker to bring onboard a person to act as producer or executive producer who has some experience in the film financing area to assist in this process.

Secondly, focus on the target audience of the film and make judgments on the film's commerciality prospects. In other words look at the revenue up side and match against the budget cost and see what it says. For instance, you have a family film budget at $30m with C level actors in your wish list; it is highly unlikely the cost to revenue will in any way match in a favorable way! It is important to then place all the elements into the film package in a professional way that addresses a realistic budget - a realistic wish list of actors/directors and an approach to potential revenue.

Thirdly, once the film package looks in reasonable order it is time to evaluate the financing options that are available and decide the best way to move forward.

Finally, the filmmaker needs to look at his financing requirements and make decisions on which of the many options best fit the film project and his own needs. This chapter goes over many of these options and, of course, there are many combinations of options available to a filmmaker which can include pre-sales, utilizing an internet crowd funding approach, equity investors, LLC option, soft money options, etc.

It is important to understand that each film project has to be evaluated as its own stand-alone project. A reasonable budget and film package needs to be prepared and then the financing options evaluated based on the filmmakers own requirements.

FILM FINANCING SOURCES

These are many and varied. Financing is often a combination of various funding avenues...... some are listed below.

- ❖ **FRIENDS, YOURSELF & FAMILY** - plus the local dentist!
- ❖ **PRIVATE FINANCING** (Equity/Loan/LLC)
- ❖ **PRE-SALES**
- ❖ **GAP FINANCING**
- ❖ **SOFT MONEY** (Government based grants/tax incentives/rebates/ shelters/tax credits/co-prod.)
- ❖ **INTERNET** (Crowd funding, etc.)
- ❖ **FILM INDUSTRY ASSISTANCE** (Post-production deals/cast-crew deferrals/equipment deals)
- ❖ **OTHER** (Negative pick-up/product placement/sponsorship)

FRIENDS, YOURSELF AND FAMILY – Plus the local dentist!

At the lowest end of the film budget scale comes the potential for a filmmaker to self-finance a film project by utilizing his own money, credit cards, family money or family friends. It is amazing how many films are funded this way and often provide the beginning to lucrative careers – from little acorns grow huge trees! It can also lead to trouble and potential bankruptcy so be very careful. In general a word to the wise – do not use your own money!!

With regard to family and friends, always stipulate to them how risky a film investment is and that they could lose the full amount. Secondly, ensure they are privy to all developments in the project both good and bad. That also means confiding with them in times of trouble as they may be able to help. Finally, even with family and friends it is best to obtain professional advice which may include an entertainment lawyer or a representative who knows the film business to help guide you.

I have produced many independent films and helped finance many others. I always used other people's money, except in one instance, that was the family film "Malaika" (aka "Tons of Trouble"). This film project was presented to me by the writer/director in 1997. I had been in the independent film business for over 10 years by then. I decided to fund the film myself and keep the film budget under $350,000. I immediately made some pre-sales and cut a deal with a post house and then went ahead and flowed my own cash into the production as I was confident that my sales agency experience would enable me to sell the film and do well. I would only recommend that course of action if you know the sales potential for the film is real and attainable. I knew that from my many years of experience and I wanted a family film so my kids could see it on UK television. I would strongly recommend any filmmakers to think twice or 10 times before investing in their own film with their own money without fully exploring sales projections. Believe me not many filmmakers do that or are even capable of knowing how to do it. This book will help all you budding filmmakers.

A much better idea is to find an investor(s) who is prepared to take the risk of financing a film project and to do that requires an enticing film project business plan.

PRIVATE FINANCING

Such a discussion should include equity financiers, loans and the PPM.LLC. To be clear, private funding in this category involves loans or equity funding from sources other than advances from distributors, pre-sales and from banks. We have discussed the private funding associated with you, your family and friends but now we will discuss investments from other investor types. Let us clarify terms often misunderstood.

Equity – An investment based on the project making profits (this needs to be defined). The investment plus return on investment comes from profits and profits only. Equity is truly risk money. Repayment is contingent on profits. Equity investments that are classed as securities are heavily regulated under state and federal law. If the investors have no control over the film project business then the investment is classed as a security. Examples of such investment/securities are stock in a corporation or limited liability companies (LLC) or partnerships.

The rule of thumb is that for every percentage point of the budget provided in equity, you should give between 0.5 percent and 0.75 percent of your profit. If the investor puts up 30 percent of your budget, you might be expected to give the investor 20 percent of the film's profit.

Equity investments can be structured in a number of ways but here are two ways:

- Limited Liability Company (LLC)
- Limited Partner in a Partnership

An investor shares in rewards and risks!!

Note: The interests of individuals that do not manage the enterprise they invest in are known as securities. There are federal and state regulations/laws designed to protect such investors against false or misleading information or lack of full disclosure.

Loan - An investment that has to be repaid no matter how the film performs - profit is not relevant. A loan has to be repaid at a specific time and has a stated interest rate that must be paid. This is a general statement. There are certain caveats to that statement, such as "nonrecourse", where the loan can only be repaid from revenue generated from the licensing of the film and only in that manner.

With private funding involving a loan and especially equity/securities a lawyer should be involved. With regard to equity investments a standard film financing deal concerns 50% for the creative and producing team and the other 50% for the investor team. Both sides share in the profits on a point's allocation. A point refers to one percent of the profits (as defined).

Simply put, to sell a security falls into categories:

Private Placement - sell directly to wealthy investors or people you know and prepare a private placement memorandum (PPM)

Public Offering - sell through brokers and prepare a prospectus.

It is important to clearly establish the order the revenue receipts from the sale of the film, ie. order of recoupment -who gets what, in what order and when and how for each party.

Private Placement Memorandum (PPM) -This is a financing vehicle often used in film funding. It strictly requires the issuer of this PPM to disclose all material information including risks to potential investors and at a minimum include:

➢ The corporate vehicle and structure, plus management details.

➢ The amount to be raised.

➢ Repayment details.

➢ The film budget and film synopsis, plus film market commerciality.

➢ The operating agreement of the corporate structure (LLC).

As you will read below, discussing sales projections and financials within the PPM for the film and the industry can be a concern should your projections not be met. An LLC (Limited Liability Company) is a common funding vehicle in the film industry. It offers limited liability protection to investors. However, a major concern with this avenue of funding relates to full compliance with applicable federal and state securities laws.

A Private Placement Memorandum (PPM) is an extremely detailed and complex document. The PPM is the legal document that governs the terms and conditions of the investment made by outside investors. The prospectus is the marketing material that film producers may use to solicit interest in the film project investment. The primary purpose of such a document is to give the film producers the opportunity to present all possible risks to potential investors. The PPM is supposed to protect the film producers in the event that the investment goes sour! That's why it's so important that the private placement memorandum be accurate and complete and meets the highest standards of full disclosure (under securities laws) to potential investors. I am no attorney but believe me the PPM must be prepared by qualified attorneys who understand those complexities very well. Therefore, such a document has to be treated with great care and diligence and can have serious results for all parties involved if not correctly prepared. Such PPMs can be a starting point for film producers considering the possibility of raising capital via a private placement.

Such a PPM may have the following statement right upfront:
"THE SHARES OFFERED HEREBY ARE HIGHLY SPECULATIVE, AND AN INVESTMENT IN SHARES INVOLVES A HIGH DEGREE OF RISK AND IMMEDIATE AND SUBSTANTIAL DILUTION FROM THE OFFERING PRICE". SEE "RISK FACTORS" AND "DILUTION."

As you see from this statement, risk is an important ingredient in full disclosure required by the film producers.

Issuing a private placement memorandum (PPM) lets your film company sell shares to "passive investors" (those who invest but take no active role in the production) in order to raise the money needed for the film project. The PPM discloses all of the risks (including the risks that you cannot find a distributor for the film and that it never achieves commercial success) associated with the project, making it difficult for investors to claim that they were not adequately warned.

PPM/FILM FUNDING.....FILMMAKERS BEWARE!

In the late 1990's, I was asked to be involved with a film that was to be funded via a Private Placement Memorandum/an LLC. My company was to be the worldwide sales agent for the film which was budgeted at about $1.2m. I read the script and also reviewed the film package (writer/director/actors/producers etc.) to be involved in the production and I reviewed the production budget. I did my due diligence on the film project.

I liked the film project and I liked the genre and pace of the script, etc. so I was happy to provide revenue estimates for the film. Those estimates were for worldwide revenue potential at a low/medium/high basis of revenue potential by each major territory worldwide. Doing such estimates of revenue potential was common place for me as I had been a sales agent for independent films for many years and I knew the film sales market very well both domestically and internationally.

I also knew that it was important to have at least one established actor of note that would help sell this film. This project had that.

Secondly, I knew the film had to have good production value and that the money of the budget had to go on screen and not all on upfront fees for the producers. Based on my review I then gave permission for my name to be included in the Private Placement Memorandum for the financing of this film project.

Some short time later, I was presented with the memorandum that looked very professional and had a quality marketing presentation of the film project. This memorandum included my company as the official sales agent for the project. In other words, it was my job to sell the film and generate revenue to pay back the investors who would subscribe to this film funding offering and generate profits for all concerned.

I read the film producers PPM and became alarmed as to the section on "Revenue Projections" and the section discussing the "Film Industry", to the point that after numerous discussions with the producers, I withdrew from the film project and asked that my company be removed from the PPM.

What was it that alarmed me so? Before I go into depth on that topic, I wish to state that the film in question went into production with funding raised via the PPM and was completed and sales were made. Unfortunately, the film lost money and the investors lost money and those investors felt that the certain parts of the PPM contents left a great deal to be desired, to the point where the investors reported the film producers to the relevant authorities and after some time those producers were arrested!!!

My second point, before I go into what alarmed me, was another PPM was handed to me recently with a similar "contents" issue and so I thought we should all discuss what alarmed me to help budding producers take care when using a PPM vehicle to raise film financing.

The "contents" issue revolves around the fact that full disclosure in these legal documents must make sense and be appropriate for the film project in hand. By this I mean, that if the film project being put forward to be invested in is an obvious low, low budget, then to discuss at length in the PPM, the film business of the major studios is not appropriate and may be interpreted as misleading. That is my contention!

Let us discuss further... In the case of the PPM just handed to me recently, the film is budgeted at $1.3m and is a family film. The PPM is looking for equity financing of $1m via the PPM. It is important to look at the following matters when reviewing such a PPM from an investor perspective, as he wishes to ensure he is having full disclosure concerning his potential investment.

So let us look at the following matters to help evaluate the film funding project:

1) Budget of the film
2) Film package – genre/actors/director/dept. heads, etc.
3) Revenue projections – both domestic & foreign
4) Marketing/distribution strategy
5) Distribution deals in place if any
6) Detailed discussion on the film industry and in particular the film business pertaining to this budget level/type of film.
7) Producers etc. - film business credentials/credits.

The PPM we are discussing states the following and based on these representations we can discuss from an investor perspective whether the PPM truly reflects full and complete disclosure and fairly represents the risks relating to the investment proposed.

1) Budget is $1.3m/Investment needed $1m
2) Film Package: Family film/no actors or director attached
3) Revenue Projections - worldwide.
   High - $36m
   Mid-Range – $18m
   Low-$6m
4) Distribution strategy – the film festival route and screenings for distributors/sales agents
5) No distribution deals in place
6) Discussion on the film industry – see below
7) Producers – credentials are ok but limited

Let us discuss item #6 - namely "Detailed discussion on the film industry" and in particular the film business pertaining to this budget level/type of film.

The PPM discusses at some length the film industry and uses extensively as a reference source the Price Waterhouse Coopers report

"Global Entertainment and Media Outlook: 2006-2010" as well as other sources including the Motion Picture Association of America and the research of Nielsen Entertainment. What concerns me about most of this data is that it relates to major studios and the fact that the data revolves around the world of theatrical releases in the USA as a major factor in the revenue stream of films.

The film to be invested in, is budgeted at $1.3m and the chance that this film will ever get a theatrical release of any sort in the US is not likely at all, yet much of the film industry discussion in this PPM is about theatrical release and not the fact that such a film will probably never get a theatrical release but will go to DVD and TV and follow the usual route of a low, low budget film. There is little if any discussion about the true world of the average low budget films made by independents in the USA and how those revenue streams come about and what the film business of the independent film is really about...just look to the AFM in November in Santa Monica.

Therefore I say BEWARE!!... when you, as a producer, use a PPM for raising film finance that you ensure that you match apples with apples and not the world of studios or large independents as a reference for investors when your film is a low, low independent film destined to be sold at the AFM directly to DVD and then to TV with no theatrical release in sight. Such references in a PPM can lead to serious consequences for all concerned. That there may be intent to mislead investors is not where you wish to go. Ask the producers who I dealt with many years ago.

In conclusion:

➢ Firstly, make sure your discussion of the film business in the PPM is appropriate to the budget level and type of film you are producing. Include reference materials that cover the film market and its revenue streams in a realistic manner.

➢ Secondly, ensure your revenue estimates are based on expected reality and not the exception. Make sure that they are conservative.

➢ Thirdly, get an attorney who is an expert in PPMs and ensure they know the film business appropriate to your film budget level and type of film product.

PRE-SALES

An in depth discussion of pre-sales is to be found in the chapter entitled "SELLING". Pre-sales are a common way to raise funding for a film project. Pre-sales are by definition the selling (licensing) of certain exploitation rights to the film in certain territories. This usually occurs before the film has gone into production. The pre-sales are part of the production funding and enable the producer to help fund the film and keep more equity available. The balance of the film production budget can be obtained by equity, loans, soft money, etc.

Generally, a producer will request the full license fee of the pre-sales to help the production budget; but, usually a buyer will provide only a 20% (or so) deposit plus the pre-sale contract. The balance will be payable on acceptable delivery. The producer must then go to an entertainment bank to be funded. Or, as in the case of a number of my films, an equity investor may demand two or three pre-sales to judge the commerciality of the film project and once signed fund them 100% as equity.

Pre-sales taken to a bank to be funded are "discounted". The bank lends the production directly and collects, once delivery is made, from the buyer. Naturally, the bank will ensure the buyer/distributor is a good credit risk and may even request the distributor to put up a letter of credit. In addition, a bank will demand a completion bond on the film production. These are all matters to be considered in the pre-sale route to help finance your film.

One final thought regarding pre-sales is that the producer must balance the need for too many pre-sales to help finance the film and leaving a number of territories still unsold to cover the revenue expectations of the other investors and any potential profit upside. Remember there is more about pre-sales in section on "SELLING".

GAP FINANCING

Gap financing is usually a loan by a bank that provides funds for the shortfall or gap between the total funding required for the film project and what has been raised to date. Such limited bank financing may allow your film to go into production by topping off your film funding!

Gap financing is a specialized niche market that requires expertise of the film industry, knowledge of distributors, sales agents, producers and current market conditions. It is inherently risky.

This financing from an entertainment bank is based on licenses pertaining to unsold territories. Each bank has a historical estimated value for a territory and they use this value to provide gap financing. Normally a bank would loan up to 20% of the production budget, collateralized by all the remaining unsold territories. The bank reviews the licenses already made with major territories and estimates of the value of the remaining unsold territories which may come from a reputable sales agent. The bank will expect to see that at least one or two of the major territories have been sold to ensure the projects commerciality and that unsold territories far exceed the gap being financed by the bank (coverage of 200/300% on the loan amount is not usual).

The bank charges premium fees and interest for such a loan. It allows a film to go into production without pre-selling more territories which may allow higher sales to be made once the film is completed.

The bank will ensure they are in first position recoupment – the bank's loan gets paid from first monies received from sales revenue. The bank will also take a security interest in the film project until the loan is paid in full and those costs are included in the loan. It is of interest to note that a number of private funds have come to the market place offering such services.

BRIDGE FINANCING VS GAP FINANCING

What is a bridge compared to a gap? Gap financing concerns the gap between your film budget total and what financing is actually in place. That gap (often under 20%) is what banks often help finance, based on remaining territories unsold sales projections. Bridge finance is all about timing. The time needed between what finance is required and when that cash will become available. This time lag often occurs when all the funding is in place and the legal side of the transactions are being completed, but due to circumstances, cash funding is required prior to the "close" of all the agreements. Bridge financing is often a last resort and can be very expensive.

BANK FINANCING – WHAT DOCUMENTS DO THEY REQUIRE?
Whenever a bank becomes involved in film financing the whole picture changes and specific needs, demands and requirements come into play that are stringent and time consuming. In my experience dealing with banks is always time consuming and it always takes more time than you think; plus, it is necessary to have an entertainment lawyer look over your paper work and the bank's contract. Don't waste your money on asking the lawyer to spend lots of time trying to negotiate with the bank to be more lenient in their requirement because the bank will want everything to ensure their position and that is that. The following is not meant to be an exhaustive list of documents banks require when involved in film funding – but, it certainly will provide a guide to the documents needed.

The following are typical requirements when dealing with banks.
➢ DOCUMENTS REGARDING OWNERSHIP OF FILM
  - Chain of Title
  - Articles of Incorporation etc. for the production co.
  - Copyright Report
  - Title/Trademark Report
  - Security Interest/Charge Reports – who has a security interest in the film?
  - Production Documents – usual production items – budget, shooting schedule, etc.
➢ DOCUMENTS REGARDING DISTRIBUTION
  - Distribution Agreement(s), etc.- Executed Agreements/Letter of Credit
  - Subordination Agreements, etc. - Bank may ask distributors for such documents.
  - Laboratory Pledge Holder Agreement- Authority from lab to bank.
➢ DOCUMENTS REGARDING COMPLETION GUARANTEE/BOND
  - Completion Agreement – executed copy
  - Completion Guarantee- agreement from bond co. in favor of bank
  - Cut-through Guarantee – bank is empowered to get payment directly from bond co./agents

- Opinion of Counsel - Obtain letter from bond co. that all is good with the film company
> INSURANCE
  - Production Package - Bank needs evidence of production insurance
  - Errors and Omissions Insurance – To ensure the copyright is in proper order, etc.
  - Certificates of Insurance - Bank will be additional named insured
> LOAN DOCUMENTS
  - Loan Agreement
  - Promissory Note
  - Security Documents – Bank has first lien of film, etc.
  - Laboratory Pledge Holder Agreement
  - Opinion of Producer/Borrower's Counsel – Letter between producer & bank stating that all is in good order

As you see, the whole process is voluminous and time consuming and the fees and cost involved can be significant; therefore, the budget size of the film has to be a major consideration as to the worth of the whole transaction.

WHAT ARE COMPLETION BONDS?

When banks are involved completion bonds are usually necessary. Completion guaranty is not really a form of financing but under certain circumstances funds from the completion guarantor can flow into the production to ensure completion of the film. A completion bond is an instrument that guarantees that the film will be completed without going over budget or schedule. Should either of these matters occur then it is the responsibility of the completion guarantor to pay from its own funds to finish the film (or repay investors in full if totally impossible to complete the film). A completion bond is often an essential part of any investor's requirements as it protects the investor from losing all of his money due to not having a product to sell. Under certain circumstances a bond company can and does take over a film production to protect its investment and complete the film. Obtaining a bond can therefore be a rigorous procedure. Having the right personnel is an important element to ensure the film production goes smoothly. A bond usually costs a small percentage (2%-6%) of an adjusted budget figure of the film, plus they usually demand a contingency line item of 10% be included in the budget.

SOFT MONEY

This particular section is highly technical, often involving legal terms and conditions, where professionals are required to obtain this type of funding. A thorough and complete understanding of global soft money would require intense study and practical experience. The intention here is to provide a summary of the main areas a filmmaker would require and an understanding that global soft money is indeed global - involving over 50 countries, each with their own rules, regulations and definitions that must be adhered to in order to obtain funds. Soft money is available in many countries including the USA and Canada.

This term is often used with a broad brush definition but it specifically should refer to its position regarding recoupment. In general, most investments take a firm stance on recoupment and expect a high order when it comes to being repaid. Soft money is thought of as being less aggressive in terms of recoupment if at all, as soft money often comes from sources that have other motivations regarding the investment. That source is often government initiated. Examples include film funds, tax incentives, rebates, etc. The motive for providing such soft money incentives is usually to attract and encourage film productions to shoot in a specific state, country, location and in so doing benefit the local communities in terms of jobs and purchases, etc. Obviously, it is more beneficial to maximize the amount of soft money a producer can obtain covering the film budget, as it leaves more in the "pot" for the other investors and profit participants to ultimately share.

Soft money can be an important and beneficial part of any film project financing. Soft money exists both in the USA and in many international countries. In most cases there has been a strong soft money market in the international arena (especially in Canada, UK, Australia, etc.) for many years, far longer than the relatively recent incentives adopted by the different US states. Soft money is truly global and effective and most beneficial to producers who wish to finance their film projects.

Note: Please understand that our discussion cannot be 100% accurate in all cases. For specific funding needs the filmmaker needs to consult a professional who is totally familiar with the soft money locations you wish to utilize.

Let us categorize global soft money into the following elements:

1) **Financial Incentives:**
   a) *Tax Benefits* - Related to government legislation providing many types of tax breaks, credits, etc.
   b) *Tax Shelters* - Complicated structures to enable individuals and companies to utilize film production spending to increase deductions. In so doing reduce income taxes of those involved with the structure.
   c) *Rebates* - Cash rebates are not upfront payments but are usually paid after production has occurred. These are usually based on a % of $ spent locally.
   d) *Direct Grants/Support* - Grants and other forms of direct support including awards are usually up-front payments and may not be repaid or recoupable.

2) **Co–Productions:** Based on multiple countries participating in film production. This structure allows a film production company to take advantage of simultaneous multiple benefits of soft money from more than one country on the same film project.

SOFT MONEY AND HOW IT WORKS

Tax Benefits - Such incentives relate to government legislation geared to diminish a tax payer's liability, a form of tax break. These incentives are designed by the various governing bodies involved to attract film company production spending to stimulate the local economy. Tax benefits come in all shapes and sizes and are used all over the world; therefore, terminology and definitions can and are varied and detailed knowledge is required and professional advice is recommended.

For the sake of simplicity and understanding we can split these benefits into two groups:

- Tax benefits for producers
- Tax benefits for investors

Producers Tax Benefits: Producer tax benefits are available in many countries including the USA and UK, etc. and are known as <u>tax credits</u>. Tax credits operate as credits against taxes owing to the state or federal government and may include income tax, sales tax or use tax.

Within this structure there is a <u>refundable tax credit</u> that is in essence a cash rebate. The production company must file a tax return in order to receive the tax refund. If the credit is in excess of the tax owed the production may receive a cash payment for the difference.

Also within this structure there is a <u>non-refundable tax credit</u> which will minimize, or reduce to zero, taxes owed but no more than that. However, any excess can be carried over to future years to help reduce taxes owed.

A <u>transferable tax credit</u> is by definition a tax credit that can be transferred. If this is allowed then any tax credit gained by the film production company can be purchased by individuals or companies and such a transfer can occur to those who have nothing to do with the film but would benefit by such a tax credit in their own taxes.

Tax credits are a valuable resource to a production company and are found all over the world as a financial incentive; however, such structures require expert professional evaluation. Legislation on these matters are constantly changing.

Investors Tax Benefits: Investors in film financing can be provided a <u>tax deduction</u> or tax allowance by the legislative bodies in order to reduce their income that is taxable -ie. Reduce the taxable income. An investor is allowed to write-off his film investment against his other taxable income, thereby reducing his taxable income, thereby reducing the tax payable.

Tax Shelters – Tax shelters are structures utilizing a tax incentive to enable individuals and companies to utilize film production spending to increase deductions. In so doing they reduce income taxes of those involved with the structure. A country may have a tax policy that wishes to encourage the development of a new area of business, such as film production. Therefore, they pass laws that enable 100% write-off of the production cost of the film to be deducted in the year the costs were incurred rather than over a period of years.

For simplicity sake the following gives you an example of how beneficial such a tax structure can be to all parties involved in the film:

- Film budget is $1m with $850,000 raised by pre-sales and equity, leaving $150,000 to be financed.
- A wealthy individual is found who has a large income tax bill due to be paid. Hypothetically, his income is $1m, with a tax rate of 45%; a tax bill of $450,000 is coming due.
- The wealthy individual is approached to purchase all the rights to the film yet to be produced for $50,000 and then hires the producer to make the film utilizing the $850,000 already raised and an additional $150,000 from his funds to make the production budget 100% funded.
- At this point the wealthy individual licenses all the rights back to the producer for an agreed piece of the net profit, which is usually a rather small amount.
- The result is that the wealthy individual has now gained 100% of the production cost of the film ($1m) as a tax deduction in the year the costs were incurred. That deduction can then be applied to any income of that wealthy individual. The result is that the wealthy individual's tax bill of $450,000 is reduced to zero. All this for the person putting up $150,000 plus $50,000 for the rights.
- The film gets made, the film producer has the rights back and the wealthy individual saves $250,000 in taxes.
- A win win for all!

This is a very simplified film example but there are many similar types of structures in place around the world. There are many variations of these structures; therefore, professional expertise is required before venturing into this type of film financing avenue.

On an international level producers and investors have benefited from tax funds. These tax funds allow more than one investor to pool their investment with other investors into a single fund entity. This entity then utilizes the tax laws of a country (eg. UK - section 48) to provide tax deductions under the law when investing in a qualifying film. Similarly, sale and leaseback structures were used for film production investments under past UK laws to benefit producers and investors alike.

Rebates - Usually rebates are not received by the qualifying production company until after production is completed and all production costs are spent. The amount of rebate is based on a percentage of production cost spent locally. This can be straight cash or a refund of local taxes paid.

These rebates can be calculated before production, based on what the production is to spend locally, so this anticipated rebate can be "banked". The production company can then receive a loan for production financing based on the "to be received" rebate. These types of rebates are common not only in the USA but in many countries.

Direct Grants/Support - Grants and awards are the simplest form of soft money. They are provided up front and are usually never to be repaid. Numerous countries have grant programs (hundreds of such programs exist) but they also come with strict rules and conditions.

Co-Productions - This is all about double dipping!! Acquiring soft money (any and all of the above soft money options described in this chapter) from one country and then getting soft money from another country on the same film – how great is that?

Governments are the biggest contributor of soft money. Numerous countries and many states in the United States have established soft money programs to encourage film production to come to their locations and shoot. Countries with the most lucrative film co-productions are Canada, Australia, New Zealand, Hungary, Germany, France, and Ireland. Many individual states of the USA are now also providing lucrative film incentives; although, the USA has no formal co-production treaties with any country.

Producers try to balance the need for creative compliance to the script and the essence of the film - but there is always the need for financing opportunities. Which will give the most benefit?

A producer can always minimize the amount of recoupable/repayable finance for a film production by utilizing as much soft money as possible from more than one country. To do this a film usually has to be set up as an official co-production between the relevant countries. A film will have to qualify as an official co-production under the very stringent requirements as stated by the relevant <u>co-production treaty</u> between the countries involved.

The essence of a co-production treaty between countries is that they treat films/production companies from each other's country the same as they would treat companies/films from their own country. In so doing the film/production companies can benefit from soft money options in treaty countries at the same time for the same film, providing the films/companies meet the strict qualifications set out in the treaty.

Such treaty provisions are strict, far reaching and involve extensive terms and conditions that must be met for a film to qualify as an <u>official co-production</u>. These provisions vary between countries. Some countries such as Canada and France have co-production treaties with many other countries, whereas, the USA has no treaties at all.

Co-Production Qualifications - Benefits from each treaty country vary. However, the qualification criteria tend to stay along the following general requirements. *Please take note* - my comments are generalities and should you venture into a co-production, producers must seek professional advice.

- *Minimum financial contribution* - Usually countries require a % financial contribution to be spent in their country.
- *Common Management & Control* - Co-producers must be independent of each other.
- *Creative Contribution* - Creative contribution should equal (approx.) the financial contribution.
- *Location* - Film must be made (including post-prod.) in the countries of the treaties involved.
- *Music* - The score (usually) must be composed by nationals or residents of treaty countries involved.
- *Credits* - Clear credit stipulation of countries involved in co-prod.
- *Qualifying Nationals* – Usually it is required that those hired are nationals or residents of participating treaty countries; however, there are exceptions especially for a leading acting role or director from a non-treaty country (ie. USA)
- *Agreement Terms* - Co-producer agreements must have clear statements on important aspects of the deal – financial/ recoupment/income/ownership, etc.

National Films - What Are They? In many countries there is a requirement that for the film to benefit from the financial incentives the film must be qualified as a National Film of that country (eg. Australia, UK). However, an official co-production side steps that requirement.

Please note - all countries in the European Union (EU) have signed up to the European Convention, which allows co-producing films the benefits for all national films in each of the EU countries.

- *Qualified Production:* Motion pictures, documentaries, specials, commercials, infomercials, etc.

- *Qualified Expense:* An expense that a state/country allows to be included in the rebate or tax credits calculation. This definition can and does vary state to state/country to country but usually includes all direct costs incurred in production (pre/prod/post) within the state/country involved.

- *Qualified Labor:* Usually includes payroll and fringes paid to a resident of the state/country involved in the film production process.

SOFT MONEY - THINGS TO BE CAREFUL OF!

➢ **Definition of Local Spending:** Understand and be clear of each state/country's rules and requirements on money spent.

➢ **Automatic vs Selective:** Fully understand what needs to be applied for and what is automatic.

➢ **Repay or No Repayment:** The rules should clearly state what is repayable via future revenues and what is free money.

➢ **Percentage?** Ensure clarity on what % are applicable for your production.

➢ **What is Required from Outside?** This is an important consideration. Many states/countries may lack crew, equipment, film infrastructure, materials, etc. and therefore costs may be incurred to bring those items in.

THE INTERNET

The internet is becoming an ever increasing important part of the distribution network, not only for independent feature films but also studios are taking notice. The internet is also playing a role as a film financing source that has developed over recent years. Like all new avenues, time will tell how influential the internet will become for both distribution as well as financing. Independent feature films have historically been funded by family money, equity, pre-sales, soft money and gap, so how will the internet change or influence that model?

Many conventional sources of funding have dried up for independent feature films; therefore, it is logical for producers to turn to the internet as a possible new source for funding. This type of solicitation is called crowd funding.

If we are to look at the motivating factors to the different types of financing it is clear to see that equity is motivated by profit; soft money by enticing production to a certain location; gap by secure cover to the loan. However, when we look at pre-sales, where sales are based on clear territory by territory licensing and a clear delineation on film rights - the internet provides a situation regarding territoriality. The internet has no such territory boundaries; therefore, will future internet financing effect the traditional financing model?

The internet has many implications for the film industry which include distribution methods, production funding sources, revenue windows, piracy and of course marketing strategy. Internet distribution is the future of the film industry. The internet will allow ease of access and vast availability of film titles at a flick of a switch – a remarkable distribution tool.

Most independent films are funded by equity, pre-sales, gap financing and, of course, soft money. Will the internet affect these sources and/or will other factors come into play. Sales and pre-sales are territory driven and the internet can significantly affect the concept of "territory". The film industry has to clearly address the fact the internet has no territory boundaries and no policing methods to control it.

CROWD FUNDING

Crowd funding (sometimes called crowd financing or crowd sourced capital) describes the collective cooperation and involvement by people who network and pool their money together, usually via the internet, in order to support efforts initiated by other people or organizations such as film financing. This term has now become part of film financing jargon. Although the true impact of this financing option is marginal at the moment - it could become material in the near future. The idea is to attract many small individual investors into film funding via the internet. If crowd funding is to work for the independent film industry it needs to appeal to investors on a level that will entice them to part with their money, namely... Greed and self-interest! So, producers need to focus on appealing to those instincts. For the price of a DVD, or even a more substantial investment, the producer has to create a demand and a return that will attract investors – big or small.

There are many examples of crowd funding all over the world. Fundable.org was an early organization and IndieGoGo, KickStarter, and RocketHub are sites that allow individuals to get involved with film projects and then allow those individuals to "donate" money. In general, they tend to be small, "mum and pop" type set-ups. In time a structure will develop that will work, but the crowd funding strategy is very much a WIP.

Some of the ways producers have tried to utilize the internet and crowd funding are:

➢ Pre-selling DVDs to investors - This seems doomed to failure as DVDs are fast becoming extinct. VOD is the future and as yet I have not seen a pre-sale of a VOD!

➢ For post-production financing - Producers needing funding to finish a project will be able to demonstrate to the public the product already made and then show investors the progress via footage, etc.

➢ Initial production funds or development financing - could work well for crowd funding as it could be direct as a form of equity replacement for "family & friends" strategy. Naturally, a good business plan and a marketing hook would be needed, but the internet could very well work for this initial funding. However, be very careful not to fall foul of the SEC who regulates investing and restricts soliciting to "qualified investors" within US borders. In general, be careful as scammers will be floating out there on the net and the general public knows this.

WARNING!
With budgets that are indeed low (less than $100,00) I think crowd funding can seriously help a filmmaker; but, please note that raising money for films can get a filmmaker into potential legal troubles (refer to my PPM/LLC financing discussion). The aspect of a "donation" based financing campaign versus an "investment" can create a legal grey area.

Sites such as KickStarter and IndieGoGo provide avenues for raising funds, especially development funds, but may be more troublesome for production funding. KickStarter offers the following outline in more detail for a typical crowd funding website. In their own words...

➢ KickStarter is a new form of commerce and patronage. In our world, the best way to inspire support is to offer people great rewards. Everyone loves limited editions, one-of-a-kinds, and fun experiences (parties, screenings, balloon rides!). Spend some time brainstorming your rewards and people will respond.

➢ On KickStarter, a project must reach its funding goal before time runs out or no money changes hands. Why? It protects everyone involved. This way, no one is expected to develop a project with an insufficient budget. Set your funding goal - aim to raise the minimum amount needed. Projects can always raise more than their goal.

➢ Can KickStarter be used to solicit investments or loans? NO - Kickstarter is a new form of commerce and patronage, not a place for investment or lending. It is donation - not investment! Projects never give up ownership or payback any funds raised on KickStarter.

➢ What percent of KickStarter projects are successfully funded? Just less than 50% - over 3,000 to date.

➢ Does KickStarter take some percentage of ownership or intellectual property? NO.

➢ Each month over a million people visit KickStarter to discover great projects, but momentum always starts with people you know.

➢ The average project is raising under $10,000.

➢ Average pledge is $68, and the most common pledge is $25.

The following is an example of what a person who donates (various levels) might get in return from a film project:

- *Pledge $5 or more* - For the price of a cup of coffee you just got a "special thanks" credit and exclusive download of the finished film before an audience sees it.

- *Pledge $10 or more* - The above perks, plus exclusive MP3's of the original score and original music.

- *Pledge $25 or more* - The above perks, plus an autographed (by filmmaker) limited edition "Film" t-shirt - likely to become a collector's item with the release of the feature film.

- *Pledge $50 or more* - For a select few, an autographed limited edition DVD of my previous film -plus all of the above perks.

- *Pledge $100 or more* - You're now an associate producer! Get film credit plus 2 tickets to LA's premiere screening of the film.

- *Pledge $1,000 or more* - Executive producer credit plus make you an extra in the film! Plus you get 2 invitations to each and every festival screening as well as for opening screening.

- And continue up the value order until they become a lead actor and director of the film…….not really!!

Crowd Funding Advantages:

- Anyone can do it! Yes anyone can create a project and place it on the net and have people donate.

- No strict rules or regulations exist with what to do with the funds raised - but make sure they go into the film project as fraud can still become a problem. Make sure that whatever was promised in return for the donation is given to the person donating.

- The donations do not have to be repaid!

- People who actually donate become "invested" in your project and can become major buzz/word of mouth contributors for your film project all the way through its life.

Crowd Funding Disadvantages:

- Be appropriate, plan and be clear what you are trying to accomplish with this activity.
- The dollar amounts of film funding are very limited in size.
- Be careful about violating any laws relating to the sale of securities, charitable fund raising or consumer fraud. Individuals must donate and have NO expectation they will share in the projects' profit or participate in the management of the project. This is a very important fact – only accept donations. Make it clear they have no involvement in the project or in the profits.
- Ensure any items promised to the individual who has donated to the project are delivered in a timely manner; otherwise the producer could be liable for consumer fraud.

FILM INDUSTRY ASSISTANCE

Film financing options are many and varied. We have discussed many of "the usual suspects" in the film funding world - equity, LLC, pre-sales, gap financing and financial incentives. However, further avenues for bridging that funding budget gap come from within the film industry itself, namely:

➢ ***Post-Production Deals*** -These types of deals are very important to low budget productions. I have used them myself a number of times. A post-production house offers their services and facilities on a deferred basis or on a discounted basis, in return for the deferral payment plus an equity stake in the net profits. As post-production covers a sizable share of a film's budget such a deal can provide a great contribution to the film being made. Certainly, in Los Angeles this practice is not unusual and in Europe I have known post houses in Germany to even take their own territory as collateral for their involvement in such an arrangement.

➢ ***Cast, Crew and Producer Deferrals*** - Is this item really film financing? The answer is yes; as it reduces the amount of finance a producer needs to go into production. Sometimes the word "deferments" is another way of saying "you will never be paid" - but that is not necessarily true. A deferment is by definition an amount or fee being delayed for payment to another time in the future. For example, an actor, director or a producer would have a fee stated in the production budget, but would agree to part of said fee being delayed for payment until the film has generated sales revenue. Such an actor deferral can often be in first place on the recoupment schedule; whereas, a producer deferral is often not paid till after a bank loan has been repaid. Such courses of action often happen in low budget films where the producer, actors and even crew accept deferments to help reduce the cash budget of the film and reduce the amount of financing needed from other sources of funding.

➤ *Production Equipment Deals* - It is not unusual to come to some form of financial arrangement with the sound mixer or lighting people or camera director of photography to have their equipment on the production with some form of partial payment upfront and the balance of the equipment rental from film revenues in an agreed order of recoupment position. These, below the line production costs, being deferred can be significant in helping reduce the cash budget of the film.

OTHER FILM FINANCING OPTIONS
NEGATIVE PICK-UPS

This book is about independent feature films; therefore, only a brief discussion is required regarding negative pick-ups. A negative pick-up is a contractual agreement ("picks up the negative"), usually between a studio and an independent producer, to acquire all rights to all territories (usually all domestic or all the world). The studio guarantees the producer that it will distribute the finished/delivered film and reimburse the agreed negative cost subject to the terms of the agreement.

This agreement allows the studio to purchase the film once it is completed. This allows the producer to present this agreement to an entertainment bank who then provides film funding based on that contract. Just as in any pre-sale agreement, it is the producer's responsibility to ensure that the studio or buyer is "bankable" (that they are good for payment on delivery) and that the entertainment bank will fund the contract.

Over the years many independent producers have come to me with stories of potential studio pick-up deals, but I have rarely seen one happen. It always reminds me about the fact that studio acquisition people constantly track new films, even low budget ones, and producers get so excited when they receive a call from a studio acquisitions department asking about their new film. They immediately run around town telling everyone that a studio is interested in their film. Unfortunately, a call from a studio is often nothing more than the acquisitions department doing their job in tracking projects. It does not mean, in 99.99% of cases, anything will ever come of it. How sad!! So do not get too excited about negative pick-up deals. You will probably never see one – another myth of Hollywood continues!!

SPONSORSHIP & PRODUCT PLACEMENT

After spending two years as VP of the Los Angeles Olympic Organizing Committee, I am well-versed in the world of sponsorship. I have also been involved in programs that utilized product placement. Their benefit can always help reduce the required budget cash requirement of a film project.

Sponsorship: Investment in-cash or in-kind, in return for access to exploitable business potential associated with an event, film or highly publicized entity.

Product Placement: Companies provide cash or in-kind services/ materials in return for screen time and/ or marketing associated with the film. For film it usually refers to a product, its brand name and/or logo appearing on screen within the film itself, rather than just an end credit. One of the most amazing films displaying product placement was, of course, "Talladega Nights" where there were over 30 products displayed.

There are a number of companies, especially in Los Angeles, that specialize in film product placement. Remember companies will need to ensure there is a clear and measurable benefit from such sponsorship or product placement.

Product Placement Companies:

Clearance Domain LLC	Valencia, CA	(800) 562-1231
Creative Entertainment Services	Burbank, CA	(818) 748-4800
Davie-Brown Entertainment	Los Angeles, CA	(310) 979-1980
Hadler Public Relations, Inc.	Glendale, CA	(818) 552-7300
HERO Entertainment Marketing, Inc.	Sun Valley, CA	(818) 764-7414
I.S.M. Entertainment, Inc.	Santa Cruz, CA	(831) 824-8001
Keppler Entertainment, Inc.	Manhattan Beach, CA	(310) 658-8000
Larry Dorn Associates/World Backgrounds	Los Angeles, CA	(323) 935-6266
Motion Picture Magic	Burbank, CA	(818) 953-7494
Norm Marshall & Associates	Sun Valley, CA	(818) 982-3505
Pier 3 Entertainment	Redondo Beach, CA	(310) 376-5115

Note: In today's world producers need to be as creative as possible regarding financing a film project. That means utilizing a hybrid film financing model. In reality that means focus on as many ways and sources to fund as are available to you; whether it be crowd funding, pre-sales, equity, gap funding, family, friends --- anything to get the job done!!

THREE FINANCING QUESTIONS YOU NEED TO UNDERSTAND:

1) **Funding**

Who is the funding party?

What is the trigger mechanism for the funding?

When is the funding due and how is it to be made?

What is the collateral if any for the investment?

What is the interest/profit term?

2) **Pay out**

How is the investment repaid?

When is the investment repaid?

What is the order of recoupment for interest/profits?

3) **Control**

Who controls the finances and who controls the creative.

KEEP IT SIMPLE STUPID!

With financing it is always best to KEEP IT SIMPLE. Simple reduces the cost, reduces the time, reduces anxiety and reduces the things that can go wrong…. because believe me in all film financing stuff things just go wrong. The knack is putting it right quickly and cheaply. Next, always solidify commitments and agreements in writing and have them signed. Do not delay. Oral agreements are always open to interpretation – in writing brings clarity to all parties. Finally, when a written agreement is to be prepared make sure you prepare the agreement and present it to the other party. Include all your understanding of the terms and conditions. The other party then responds to your agreement and further revisions flow through you first.

INVESTORS

KNOW YOUR INVESTOR

Film financing is never easy and projects can be financed in many ways. But one thing is for certain, a producer/filmmaker must understand the financier/investor motivation. What do they want out of the deal? For instance, a bank that provides gap financing is looking for fees and collateral to cover principal and interest. An equity player may be after a large return from a risky investment colored by having fun on the set and being involved with the glamor of the film business. On the other side, a government provides grants and incentives to stimulate local employment and business in their state or country.

RECOUPMENT - WHO GETS WHAT WHEN?

The favorite question all investors want to know is - when am I getting my money back? That is not only a function of time, but also where in the order of recoupment is that investor as revenue flows in from film sales. The order of recoupment is an important element in the agreement between producer and investor. This recoupment schedule is finalized at the time of financing and agreed by all parties including profit participants. As sales revenue flows in from deals made all over the world there is a specific delineated order of pay out which states exactly what dollars go where and to whom. If a bank is involved they usually go first in the pecking order until they are paid off. For more details on order of recoupment go to the chapter on "SELLING".

HOW DO YOU FIND INVESTORS?
Investors are everywhere. I once meet an investor at a hairdressing salon opening... Another I met on a plane... Another I met at the Super Bowl... Another I met at a party... Another I met and was introduced to by friends. Get the picture? Just learn to search them out – they are everywhere.

APPROACHING AN INVESTOR – THE PITCH
Naturally, from the filmmaker hunting money, a potential investor needs to see enthusiasm for your film project tempered by a good understanding of the film industry. This means be prepared with a clear and detailed business plan. With investors, always be honest and be on the conservative side regarding financials. Be professional, respectful and ensure once the potential investor expresses interest you follow up with a full exploratory meeting – then off you go.

Ensure that your business plan encompasses:
➢ How much you want?
➢ When you want it?
➢ How you plan to return it?
➢ When you will return it?
➢ What guarantees are you giving if any?
➢ What is his return on investment and when will he get it?
➢ What experience do you have in the industry?
➢ And of course, a full and detailed business plan.

Never even think about pitching to an investor until you are 100% sure about the content and approach of your pitch. There are many approaches to pitching your film project to an investor, but here are some of my thoughts:
➢ Always be professional – both in manner and attire.
➢ What is the film about? – Have a clear concise but passionate appreciation you can extol to the investor. Describe the story and explain why you want to make this film. Provide him a synopsis of the film story.

> Why make this film now? – It is important to express to investor why the film should be made now.
> Make the investor feel comfortable that his investment will not be wasted and that the film will be made and sold.
> Who will benefit from this film?
> Understand the investor and try to understand his motivation for investing in the film.
> Be engaging, interesting, passionate and entertaining.
> Know how much you want from your investor. Know how he will get his money back and when and with what profit. But, also inform him about risks – do not mislead or paint an unrealistic financial picture.
> Highlight your film business credentials and experience and any other assets you feel appropriate - eg. Actor or director interested, plus any distributor interested.
> If possible have marketing materials to show – sell sheet/ artwork/trailer – even though your film has not been made you can provide the investor a visual image of how yours is to look.
> Have a professional business plan prepared.
> Do not be pushy or act like a used car salesman. Be direct, affirmative and polite.
> A commitment on the first meeting is great, but more likely the investor will want to consider your pitch. Therefore, set a time for a second meeting – at that time try to close a deal.

DEALING WITH INVESTORS – IS IT REAL?
A skill all filmmakers/producers want to acquire and acquire quickly is the ability to evaluate whether an investor and/or the investment is real. Over the years I have been approached by many supposed equity financing deals. To say only a very small fraction of them turn out to be real is an understatement. So the following are a few tips to help you limit the amount of time you might waste:
> Get as much detail upfront about the money source as possible so you can quickly evaluate. Items you should inquire about include - What amounts? How much? Which bank is it in? What films have they funded before? What entertainment lawyers do they use?

➢ Are you dealing with a broker or a principal? Get to the principal ASAP.

➢ Google both broker and principal and also ask for industry references so you can check.

➢ Can you verify funds? Be careful about letters and bank statements as they may be copies. Ask for permission to talk directly with a bank officer to verify funds. Verification of funds will speed up the process of knowing if they are real. Stalling or providing convoluted stories should raise a red flag.

➢ Asking for money upfront, either for a fee or expenses, is another red flag.

THE CON ARTIST - OR WHAT?

Filmmakers and newbie producers be aware of the film financier con artist. These guys will eat your time alive and you will get nowhere fast. You will lose your mind and possibly money if you are not careful. These people - some are well meaning and are just fools, some think they have financing sources but are just hopeful wannabees or dreamers and others are just straight sharks trying to relieve you of money and your senses. I have met them all! They basically state that they have direct access to potential film investors and they can direct these investors to your film. Naturally they want something in return. They will negotiate all the terms, etc. with the investor on your behalf.

Over many years I have met many con artists, schemers, charlatans, etc. – they all have certain traits and mannerisms that I will describe to you - so take note:

➢ Always ask for credentials (and verify them) which will include what financing they have done before.

➢ Ask for detailed description of the financing they are proposing.

➢ Ask for their driver's license, then Google them.

➢ If they ask for payments (or expenses) upfront - run!

➢ If the financing schemes they propose are elaborate then be careful, especially, when they start using such words as "letters of credit", "offshore banks", and "escrow accounts". It would always be easier to just provide the funds to "x" rather than do this convoluted transaction flow.

> Never trust someone who says "trust me".

It never ceases to amaze me how many people waste so much of a filmmakers time with bogus financing schemes – is it they just need the attention?

THE BUSINESS PLAN

This document can make or break your chances of ever getting your film made -so please take note! A business plan is a must if you require financing from sources other than yourself or immediate family/friends. To acquire financing from an independent source certain clear stipulations have to be made in order to entice that investor to invest in your film project.

A business plan is a document which clearly identifies your understanding of where your project fits into the film industry and the market it is targeted to. It should state the financial requirements of the venture; what is required from the investors; how they are to be repaid; what compensation they will receive and when and from where. Other areas within the document will include the experience of the management team and a detailed analysis of the film industry in general and the sales market the film is made for in particular.

This document is very important to independent investors and must be professional, well presented and clear. I have prepared many film business plans - some large documents, some abbreviated documents. At university, I teach how to prepare these documents, which includes marketing aspects and financing requirements for general industry as well as for the film business.

It is a well-known fact that getting the money and paying it back is the most difficult aspect of independent filmmaking – actually shooting and making the film is the easiest part!

A business plan is a road map on where you want to go and how you intend to get there. Therefore, a filmmaker should ask themselves certain questions an investor might wish to ask them before investing in a film project. Such questions could be:

> Who are you and what experience do you have in the film industry?
> Why should I invest in your film at all? What is the risk?

➢ What is my collateral? Are there any signed sales/distribution deals in place?

➢ How much do you want? When do you want it? How do you want it? – Cash of course!

➢ How do I get my money back? When and by what means?

➢ How do you know the sales potential and whether it is achievable?

➢ What profit will I make and when will I get it?

➢ Who controls the money?

The following sections should be an integral part of your film business plan:

➢ *Executive Summary* - I know this will sound odd, but the first section of a business plan namely, the executive summary, is that part you write last. Why? This is truly a succinct summary of all the major points of the plan with a clear objective and focus on what you wish to obtain from an investor. Each section of the plan should be briefly and clearly stated. Please ensure you state your intentions and motivations – your own business philosophy, your own mission statement.

➢ *Company & Management* - What is the legal set up of your company and what is its function? Provide a full description of the management team with responsibilities stated. Resumes of principals are important, especially if relevant to the film industry.

➢ *The Film* - Provide a full description of the film(s) that financing is required for. Identify any positive aspects of the project including any known actors or director or from a book, etc. Provide evidence of your competitive advantage.

➢ *The Film Industry* - An overview of the industry is required. Make sure that this overview is up to date and covers the industry relevant to your type and budget level of film. If your film is low budget then please ensure you provide a detailed account of that area of the industry. Please refrain from inferring your film is a studio film and that once completed it will get studio distribution and a major theatrical release. So often, I see business plans describe in glorious detail how studio films perform, etc. when the film in the plan has a budget under $250,000. The film industry does include the studios, but ensure your description is balanced and not misleading. Most likely your film is an independent feature and will have very little to do with the world of studios and major theatrical releases. When discussing independent films ensure you describe the domestic and foreign markets and the various rights (theatrical/DVD/TV) in particular and the windows involved and the potential revenue to be accessed.

➤ *The Market* - This section should describe the market that your film is targeting and why there is a market for your film(s). Identify similar films and their success and how your film will avoid failure and be a success. Identify your selling points that will ensure buyers, both domestic and foreign, will embrace your product. Describe your research into the commerciality of your product. Usually with low budget independent films the revenue base will be DVD and TV worldwide.

➤ *Marketing/Distribution Strategy* - Describe in detail your approach to marketing the film and how you intend to distribute the film worldwide. THIS IS VERY IMPORTANT. Provide detailed analysis about your evaluation of the options – whether they are to sign a sales agent or go to film festival or try your own DIY distribution via direct to consumer DVD distribution or any hybrid of available options. Clearly discuss your marketing materials prepared, such as sell sheets, artwork, and trailers to assist in attracting distributors. In this section it would be beneficial to have sales projections/ assumptions included. THIS IS IMPORTANT. Ask a sales agent to prepare revenue projections for your film project for both domestic and foreign. Make sure the necessary assumptions are clearly stated to avoid any misunderstanding. These are projections based on the film package and budget and that the film is not yet completed.

Financial forecasting is one of the most important elements of a business plan. It requires professionalism and industry knowledge. Key elements to include are:

- Domestic Theatrical Revenue – if applicable
- Domestic TV & DVD Revenue
- Foreign Revenue – all rights
- Total Revenue

- Negative Costs
- Marketing/Prints and Ads – if applicable
- Total Costs
- Gross Profits
- Distributor Fees
- Cash Flows
- Financial Assumptions

Financing Requirements:

- How much you want?
- When you want it?
- How you plan to return it?
- When will you return it?
- What guarantee s are you giving if any?
- What is the return on investment and when will they get it?

BUSINESS PLAN BARE ESSENTIALS

Ensure that you present a plan that is competent, well prepared and well presented. It must be professional. I suggest between 15 – 20 pages. Keep photos and graphs to a reasonable amount. Ensure you have "substance" in your plan – namely, clear statements about the commerciality of your film, extensive discussion on your approach to marketing/distribution. Have clear and reasonable financials/sales projections for your film - not a studio blockbuster!

An understanding of the film industry is a must. You are presenting cash flows and profit statements based on cost outflows and cash inflows from many revenue sources based on your timing and projections of licensing deals for the various rights of your film project over a period of time. Besides a clear projection of amounts and timing of pre-production, production, and post-production costs, the plan will require a detailed analysis of revenue - territory by territory, including rights projected to be sold. This, thereby, provides a quarter by quarter financial picture for the investor for at least three years or even five years. Naturally, your business plan will show a profit. Though in today's world of transferable tax credits and rebates the cash flow statements might become more complex, they should still show a profit. However, these statements are always based on revenue projections (hopefully provided by a sales agent professional) on a film yet to be produced, so in the real world most independent films do not live up to the expectations of the projections made in the plans. Utilize information/data you have accumulated on similar films and similar budget levels to support your projections; but, please do not state that because "Paranormal Activity" did $100m in the box office on a mini low budget your low budget film will follow. That is terribly misleading and could get you in a lot of trouble (see section on PPM funding). That is just reality ladies and gentlemen! Rarely do filmmakers start off wanting to make a bad film – it just happens that way!

As accurate film industry data as possible is required; therefore, using a sales agent is the best bet. Information can also be obtained via www.showbizdata.com. The trade paper, Hollywood Reporter, also provides a detailed analysis of sales price projects, territory by territory, for independent films in their "bumper" issue at the AFM, every year.

Note: Remember when you discuss data make sure that it relates to the budget level of your film and that it is not data relating to studio films.

It is important to clearly stipulate all your assumptions, and there will be many, that have been incorporated into the business plan. Try to be conservative and realistic in your financial projections.

SIX IMPORTANT ELEMENTS OF A SUCCESSFUL FILM BUSINESS PLAN:

1) Look Professional – please! - Your film business plan is your ticket to stardom! ...well maybe. No matter what, your business plan must look and feel professional. It must be well presented, bound, well written with quality graphs/diagrams and with quality paper and printing. First impressions count.

2) Generic vs Specific....be different - To many plans come from generic templates and they all begin to look the same but with different titles. Make an effort to customize your plan to suit your film and your vision. But, ensure all the necessary material/information is still included. Also, make it reasonably entertaining and NOT boring – Someone has to read this stuff!

3) Always Too Long...always - Most plans are way too long. Rule of thumb is 15 – 20 pages, but you can have attached supporting appendix with more material for informational purposes.

4) Marketing/Distribution...so limp! - Again we see generic statements about marketing and distribution, but it is not specific to what you want to do and how you plan to achieve it. Describe in detail your marketing plan and approach (posters/trailers/sell sheets/ YouTube/social networking/publicity/website/magazine interviews etc.). Be specific how you intend to acquire distribution – outline a strategy. This strategy may be using a sales agent or going the film festival circuit or trying to do DIY via DVD direct to consumers, etc. Provide detail specific to what you want to achieve.

5) Compare to Blockbusters – NO! - Please enough of how your little low, low budget film is another "Paranormal Activity". Be realistic and show the investor reasonable revenue projections from domestic and foreign sales, broken down by rights, from a professional sales agent.... Not the $100m box office from a similar blockbuster you pulled from the trades.

6) Supporting Materials – lack of? - Here is where you can shine and show the investor how much thought and effort you have put into your project. A must is to have a short video teaser/trailer – highly effective presentation tool. Other items to include in this area are copies of your website pages, your Facebook page, your sell sheet, cash flow projections, photos from your trailer, publicity material, articles, magazine interviews, etc. Have available a short power point presentation of the main points of your project. One thing I also recommend is to have a concise and clear informational ONE SHEET that has all the necessary information about the project – all on one page, a super summary. This can provide you with a quick attack approach and get an investors attention.

WHAT IF AN INVESTOR OFFERS YOU 50% OF YOUR BUDGET AND SAYS GO MAKE THE FILM FOR THAT DOLLAR AMOUNT – WHAT DO YOU DO?

What are your options? A producer can say thank you and say no, I need the budget amount! Or...No, I need to find more cash to get closer to the budget figure! Or... is it more realistic to say yes, and let's get looking at the budget to see where we can reasonably cut without destroying the integrity of the film itself. I have, on a number of occasions, been faced with that kind of dilemma. One realizes early that getting any type of financing in today's climate is a blessing so find a way to make it work but ensure the deal points make sense – don't give away the store, but at the same time do not cut off your nose to spite your face.

WHEN IS A DEAL, A GOOD DEAL?

So private financing has been offered on your film project – but, what is the deal? What are the terms and conditions attached to the financing being offered? Let us discuss the various elements that will come into play when discussing a deal for film funding. In the section above I outlined briefly the important points and here we shall expand:

- How much is being offered and in what manner – cash or line of credit or...?
- How much do you need to make the film – what is the true film cash budget?
- When you do you need the funding – cash flow requirements?
- How do you plan to return it – what is your strategy for distribution/marketing?
- When will you return it – timing/order of recoupment?
- What guarantees are you giving if any - against what rights or other collateral?
- What is his return on investment and when will he get it - net profit/interest?

EXAMPLES - FILM FINANCING STRUCTURES AT VARIOUS BUDGET LEVELS:

❖ **Film Budget #1: $25,000**
Development – Producer money $2,000
Production - Private/family equity $10,000
Production – Deferrals – actors, crew, equipment $6,000
Production – Pre-sale $10,000 sale / deposit cash $2,000
Post-Prod - Posthouse deferral deal $5,000

❖ **Film Budget #2: $200,000**
Development – Producer money $5,000
Production – Private Equity $100,000
Production - Pre-sales $50,000
Production- Deferred fees $25,000
Post-Prod – Post house deal - $20,000

❖ **Film Budget #3: $1m**
Development - Private equity $20,000P
Production - Soft money $150,000
Production - Pre-sales banked $300,000 – two territories sold
Production – Bank Gap – sales agent estimates $180,000
Production – Private Equity $350,000

❖ **Film Budget #4: >$1m**
Equity Investor $1m
Pre-sales $1m (Three/four territories sold)
Actor/producer deferrals $250,000
Soft money $1m (Canada plus TV deal)
Bank gap + interest $500,000

SOFT MONEY – GLOBAL PERSPECTIVE

Soft money is a valuable resource to any producer who has the knowledge and flexibility to take advantage of the benefits - especially in the world of co-productions.

The economic downturn has affected many global film incentive programs. They tend to be government inspired and funded, so political pressure to cut back is a reality. The recent inclusion of film incentives from the US Federal government and the numerous US states is encouraging.

Many of the programs from well-established co-production treaty countries such as Canada, Australia, UK and Germany appear to be moving forward and in place. New film incentives are emerging from Asia namely, South Korea, Singapore and Taiwan as they see the potential - both as a production partner and a shooting location.

To maximize the benefits of the various treaties, service deals and co-production opportunities a producer must identify the most lucrative incentives from a global dinner table. A producer must look at the film script, its locations, and the budget and decide where best to film and how best to acquire the most financial incentives. Certainly, the German model is very lucrative and, of course, Canada has for many years been a target for co-productions. The ability to improve the incentive package by having a co-production between two countries, where one country has the actual shoot and the other country has the post-production works well - eg. Utilize the UK tax credit and the German incentives. A general comment is that incentives are best put together when those incentives are dis-similar in nature – eg. One country does the shoot, the other post. UK and Hungary do well as they are very different incentive packages.

Example - "Fifty Dead Men Walking"

This film was a UK-Canadian (Vancouver) co-production. The writer/ director was Canadian and key crew and cast were Canadian. The shoot was in the UK and the post was done in Vancouver. Telefilm Canada supported the film and a Canadian TV sale was also made. In Canada the film accessed both federal and provincial Canadian incentives. In the UK, the film accessed the UK tax credit, plus financial support from Northern Ireland Screen for shooting in Belfast. The film passed the cultural test of both countries.

One of the areas that always causes concern to producers is trying to turn the financial film incentives into hard cash, especially if they can be utilized as part of production funding upfront. Governments are the main instigator and provider of soft money; therefore, it would seem reasonable that financial institutions and banks would be positive in "banking" tax credits, etc. for producers and turning them into hard cash. It is usual for producers to locate and work with banks that are involved in entertainment banking. Certainly the AFMA will provide a list of such banks.

USA - STATE BY STATE- FILM INCENTIVES

The *most attractive* US film production incentive programs are:
- ➤ 40% Michigan film production credit
- ➤ 40% Puerto Rico Law 362 tax credit
- ➤ 30% New York State Film Production Credit
- ➤ 30% Louisiana Motion Picture Investor Tax Credit
- ➤ 30% Connecticut Digital Media & Motion Picture Tax Credit
- ➤ 25% Massachusetts Motion Picture Tax Incentive
- ➤ 25% New Mexico Film Production Tax Rebate
- ➤ 20%-25% California Film & Television Tax Credit Program
- ➤ 20% Georgia Entertainment Industry Investment Act

US FEDERAL SECTION 181

This is the corner stone of the US film production incentive program from a federal level. Section 181 allows producers or active financial participants to take an immediate tax deduction, rather than writing off the costs over a period of years, for the first $15m of US production costs for qualifying film or television productions. The first $20m of costs can be immediately deducted if the project is made in a designated low income or distressed area of the country. At least 75% of the total compensation expended on the production must be for services performed in the US.

Section 181 has been modeled on the European incentives such as the UK's no longer working sale-and-leaseback scheme. However, it has had its problems living up to expectations, especially for independent film companies. Production companies can and do pass the deduction on to investors.

THE YES AND NO'S OF USA PRODUCTION INCENTIVE PROGRAMS BY US STATE -

The following discussion points are addressed:

➢ What the program provides?
➢ How does producer access the money?
➢ Is the money upfront or back–end?
➢ Can other territories incentives also be used in conjunction?
➢ How stable is the program?
➢ Producer's likes & dislikes?
➢ Films that have used the program?
➢ Contact Information

What the Program Provides.

Michigan: Provides a refundable, assignable tax credit of up to 40% of the amount of a production company's expenditures incurred producing a film or other media entertainment in Michigan - with an extra 2% if filming is in one of the state's 103 "core communities." Above and below the line salaries are included.

Puerto Rico: Provides 40% transferable tax credit on a project's payments to Puerto Rican entities or residents, including expenditures for equipment, crew and travel for all production expenses. Above-the-line payments to non-residents are not included.

New York: Provides a refundable 30% tax credit on qualified production costs incurred by features and TV movies or series which shoot at a qualified state production facility. The Made in New York program provides an additional 5% refundable credit on qualified expenditures for productions shooting within the five boroughs of New York City.

Louisiana: Offers a 30% transferable tax credit for total Louisiana production expenditures including costs for services performed in the state by residents and non-residents alike. There is an additional 5% labor tax credit for Louisiana residents.

Connecticut: Transferable tax credit of up to 30% on qualified film and digital media production, pre-production and post-production costs incurred in Connecticut. Covers above the line salaries up to an aggregate of $20m per production.

New Mexico: Provides a 25% refundable tax credit on all direct film, TV, documentary and video game production and post-production expenditures. The state also offers loans of up to $15m per project.

California: There are two levels of tax credits. A 20% credit on qualified expenses for feature films budgeted between $1m and $75m, TV movies/ mini-series/cable TV series. The second credit level is a 25% tax credit on qualified expenses for truly independent films budgeted between $1m and $10m. Qualified expenses will include all below-the-line costs but not above-the-line wages or purchase of story rights. Projects must spend 75% of their production days or total production budget in California.

How Does Producer Access the Money?

Michigan: Once all production work in Michigan has been completed the production company requests a post-production certificate specifying the amount of the credit from the Michigan Film Office. The company must then file a state tax return at the end of its tax year to claim the credit. This is transferable so it can be assigned to anyone.

Puerto Rico: Requires a licensed film entity to make payments to Puerto Rico residents. Once production is completed and the costs verified a letter certifying the credit is issued and the credit can then be used or sold.

New York: The production company must apply for conditional approval of a project before the start of principal photography. Tax credits are then applied to the company's New York State and/or New York City tax returns for the year in which the production was completed. If the amount of the state credit earned exceeds any state tax owed, the excess is refunded.

Louisiana: During or after production – verify costs.

Connecticut: Costs have to be verified. A tax credit voucher is issued. Credits are non-refundable, but may be sold or transferred to third parties.

New Mexico: The project is registered before production and a script submitted. After production and the project have met all New Mexico financial requirements, an application for tax credit is submitted. Once taxes filed, any excess credit over tax liability is refunded.

California: Applications must be submitted at least 30 days before start of principal photography. If the project is approved, the producer gets a credit allocation letter stating amount of credits reserved. On completion of the production a tax credit certificate is issued. Credits applied to income tax liability are not refundable. Tax credits issued to an independent film may be transferred or sold to a third party.

Is the Money Upfront or Back–End?

Michigan: Back-end

Puerto Rico: Back-end

New York: Back-end

Louisiana: During and after production.

Connecticut: Back-end

New Mexico: Back-end

California: Back-end

Note: Although credits are back-end, often these credits can be banked and loans issued to help upfront production costs.

Can Other Territories Incentives Also Be Used In Conjunction?

Michigan: Yes

Puerto Rico: Yes

New York: Yes

Louisiana: Yes

Connecticut: Yes

New Mexico: Yes

California: Yes, but note the 75% rule.

How Stable is the Program?

All these programs are stable until they become unstable! These programs are government operated and are, therefore, totally open to change, amendment and cancellation at any time. So always check.

Producer's Likes & Dislikes

Likes:

Michigan: Large % incentive program.

Puerto Rico: The island has exotic locations and is a US territory. Program is easy to use.

New York: Great city for locations. It offers plenty of studio space, equipment suppliers, crews, locations and actors, etc.

Louisiana: Well established and it works.

Connecticut: Above-the-line covered.

New Mexico: Refundable tax credit, so is like a cash rebate.

California: In February 2009 California finally agreed to incentives.

Dislikes:
Michigan: Production crews and studio stages are in short supply.
Puerto Rico: The incentive does not cover above-the-line payments to non-residents and they have limited production facilities.
New York: How stable is the program?
Louisiana: Shreveport, one of the state's main production facilities, is not that popular.
Connecticut: The above-the-line cap.
New Mexico: Limited post-production facilities.
California: Above-the-line costs do not qualify and there are certain caps.

Films That Have Used the Program
Michigan: "Up In the Air", "Red Dawn"
Puerto Rico: "The Men Who Stare At Goats"
New York: "Julie & Julia", "Sherlock Holmes"
Louisiana: "The Curious Case of Benjamin Button"
Connecticut: "Confessions of a Shopaholic"
New Mexico: "Terminator Salvation", "The Book of Eli"
California: "Dinner for Schmucks"

Contact Information:
Michigan: www.michiganfilmoffice.org.
Puerto Rico: www.puertoricofilm.com
New York: www.nylovesfilm.com
Louisiana: www.louisianaentertainment.gov
Connecticut: www.ctfilm.com
New Mexico: www.nmfilm.com
California: www.film.ca.gov

The following are the websites that will provide detailed Information on other US states that provide production incentives:
Alaska: www.alaskafilm.org
Arizona: www.azcommerce.com/film
Florida: www.filminflorida.com
Hawaii: www.hawaiifilmoffice.com
Illinois: www.commerce.state.il.us
Iowa: www.traveliowa.com/film
Missouri: www.missouridevelopment.org

Massachusetts:	www.mafilm.org
New Jersey:	www.njfilm.org
Pennsylvania:	www.filminpa.com
Rhode Island:	www.film.ri.gov
South Carolina:	www.filmsc.com

THE YES AND NO'S OF GLOBAL SOFT MONEY PROGRAMS BY FOREIGN COUNTRY

The following are details of some of the more important countries that offer attractive production incentives. Please note that in the majority of these countries the production incentives have some form of requirement - namely cultural, artistic, and contribution/spending. These requirements are considerably more complex and fundamental than any requirement in the USA state programs to the project receiving the incentives. Therefore, it is highly recommended that the producer/filmmaker thoroughly understand all the rules and, if necessary, seek professional help.

It is also important to understand that the various the various financial incentives (local, regional, state) can often be combined. Also, different countries benefits can be combined to provide additional benefits; but, let it be understood that these international country subsidies and incentives are complex and tend to change over time and the requirements must be followed. The local governmental film offices should always be contacted to ensure the most up to date information is reviewed.

BRIEF SUMMARY DESCRIPTION ON THE LEADING INTERNATIONAL PRODUCTION FINANCIAL INCENTIVE PROGRAMS (Soft Money) BY COUNTRY

The following discussion points are addressed:
- ➤ What the program provides?
- ➤ How does producer access the money?
- ➤ Is the money upfront or back–end?
- ➤ Is there a cultural or other requirement?
- ➤ Can other territories incentives also be used in conjunction?
- ➤ Producer's likes & dislikes?
- ➤ Films that have used the program?

➢ Contact Information

Note: All these programs are stable until they become unstable! These programs are government operated and are therefore totally open to change, amendment and cancellation at any time. So always check!

CANADA

Canada is one of the most important film centers in the world with over 53 co-production treaties. Not only are there federal incentives, but also generous provincial/regional incentives. Plus, they have excellent production facilities, crew and talent. Both the federal and provincial tax credits are complimentary. For example, the Ontario tax credit (25%) and the federal tax credit (16%) can be combined for a maximum rate of up to 37% of the qualified labor cost. Also, the Canadian tax credits are even more favorable for official co-productions than a straight location service shoot. Therefore, it is common practice for non-US shoots to go to Canada as a co-production to take advantage of those beneficial terms. There are three main film production centers in Canada: Vancouver, Toronto and Montreal.

Federal Tax Credits:

➢ **25%** Canadian Film or Video Production Tax Credit (CPTC)
➢ **16%** Film or Video Production Services Tax Credit (PSTC)

Provincial Tax Credits:

➢ **65%** Manitoba Film And Video Production Tax Credit
➢ **45%** Saskatchewan Film Employment Tax Credit (SFETC)
➢ **35%** Quebec Film Production Tax Credit (QFPTC)
➢ **35%** Film Incentive British Columbia (FIBC)
➢ **35%** Ontario Film and Television Tax Credit (OFTTC)
➢ **25%** Alberta Film Development Program (AFDP)
➢ **25%** BC Production Services Tax Credit
➢ **25%** Film Nova Scotia Tax Credit Program
➢ **25%** Ontario Production Services Tax Credit (OPSTC)
➢ **25%** Quebec Tax Credit for Film Production Services (QPSTC)

What he Federal Programs Provide?

There are two federal programs and numerous provincial programs. The two federal are:

- *25% Canadian Film/Video Production Tax Credit (CPTC)* - For Canadian producers and official co-productions. Provides 25% of qualified Canadian labor costs no greater than 60% of cost of production.
- *16% Film/Video Production Services Tax Credit (PSTC)*

How Does Producer Access the Money?
Canadian producers apply to CAVCO

Is the Money Upfront Or Back–End?
Back-end – based on tax return.

Is There a Cultural or Other Requirement?
For co-productions, there must be a treaty, then eligible with Canadian content rules and the points system. For the PSTC there is no cultural test.

Can Other Territories Incentives Also Be Used In Conjunction?
Yes – especially for co-production.

Producer's Likes & Dislikes
Likes:
Generous incentives.
Clear and been around a long time.
Good facilities and crews/talent.

Dislikes:
Remove the "net of assistance rule" regarding federal tax credit on labor costs as this reduces value.

Films That Have Used the Program
"Fifty Dead Men Walking"

Contact Information
Robert Soucy, director, CAVCO, Canadian Heritage
Web: www.pch.gc.ca/cavco; www.cra.gc.ca/filmservices

The following is a brief summary of the more leading Canadian Provincial Film Incentive programs:
British Columbia (Vancouver):
- *35% Film Incentive British Columbia (FIBC) Tax Credit* – Tax credit, 35%, is based on qualified British Columbia labor costs for Canadian or treaty co-productions. Other tax credits include a bonus of 12.5% for productions outside the Vancouver area, training tax credits plus a 15% credit for using BC based digital animation/VFX facilities. Back-end money. Web: www.bcfilm.bc.ca

- *25% BC Production Services Tax Credit* - Tax credit, 25%, is based on qualified British Columbia labor costs for Canadian or treaty co-productions. Other tax credits include a bonus of 6% for productions outside the Vancouver area, training tax credits plus a 15% credit for using BC based digital animation/VFX facilities. Back-end money via tax return. Web: www.bcfilm.bc.ca

Ontario (Toronto)

- *35% Ontario Film and Television Tax Credit (OFTTC)* – Refundable tax credit, 35% of qualifying costs net of assistance. First-time producers can access 40% on the first c$240,000 of qualifying labor. Producers can also receive a regional bonus rate of 10% for filming outside the Greater Toronto Area. Back-end money via tax return.
- *25% Ontario Production Services Tax Credit (OPSTC)* – Based on 25% of qualifying costs spent in Ontario, which includes production services, equipment rentals and travel within the province. Other tax credit adds 20% rebate on qualifying labor costs for digital animation or digital visual effects in Ontario. Web: www.omdc.on.ca

Quebec (Montreal):

- *35% Quebec Film Production Tax Credit (QFPTC)* - Tax Credit, 35%, is based on qualified Quebec labor costs with Quebec producer and co-productions. Other tax credits include a bonus of 10% for productions outside the Montreal area. Also, a 10% credit for eligible visual affects costs. Back-end money via tax return.
- *25% Quebec Tax Credit for Film Production Services (QPSTC)* - 25% of qualifying costs spent in Quebec and designed for service productions. Other tax credit adds 5% on qualifying costs for visual effects in Quebec. Web: www.sodec.gouv.qc.ca

Contact information for other Provincial Film Incentive programs:
- ➤ **Alberta -**   www.culture.alberta.ca/filmdevelopment
- ➤ **Manitoba -**   www.mbfilmmusic.ca
- ➤ **Nova Scotia -** www.filmnovascotia.com
- ➤ **Saskatchewan -** www.saskfilm.com

UNITED KINGDOM (UK)

In 2006 the old sale and leaseback program was replaced with the film tax-relief system. Films qualify as British either through an official co-production treaty (treaties include Australia, Canada, India and France), or by having 16 or more points in a cultural test. The test comprises four sections: cultural content, cultural contribution, cultural hubs and cultural practitioners. Many international filmmakers choose to shoot outside London as the UK's regions offer very attractive incentives.

What the Program Provides?

A tax credit of 20% is available on a maximum of 80% of qualifying expenditure on the UK production spend of a British qualifying film (budgets more than £20m), if it forms at least 25% of the film's total expenditure. For films with a budget of under £20m, producers can claim a deduction of 100% with a payable tax credit of 25%.

How Does Producer Access the Money?

It must be a "British" film and the production company must be responsible for the film and file all expense documentation.

Is the Money Upfront or Back–End?

File for tax credit as costs are incurred then it gets processed for payment.

Is There a Cultural or Other Requirement?

Yes – it must be "British". If it is an official co-production then it is eligible. Culture test has four elements with minimum of 16 points out of 31.

Can Other Territories Incentives Also Be Used In Conjunction?

Not easy as tax credit applies to UK spend only - but possible.

Producer's Likes & Dislikes

Likes:

User friendly.

Excellent studio and technical facilities.

Dislikes:

No encouragement for co-productions.

Cash flowing tax credits have a cost to be cashed.

'Used and consumed in the UK' rule.

No post-production incentive.

Contact Information

UK Film Council: www.ukfilmcouncil.org.uk/qualifying

UK Regional Funds:
These funds often work in tandem with the UK tax credit, are valuable producer resources and can provide valuable funding. They usually involve shooting in the region and certain spending is required in the region. It is usual also, that although classed as soft money. These funds are equity investments and, therefore, should be viewed as investors and expect recoupment although favorable terms appear the norm.

➢ Screen Yorkshire –
  Yorkshire, Humberside   www.screenyorkshire.co.uk
➢ Northern Ireland Screen   www.northernirelandscreen.co.uk
➢ Scottish Screen   www.scottishscreen.com
➢ Wales Creative IP Fund   www.financewales.co.uk
➢ Film Agency for Wales   www.filmagencywales.com
➢ EM Media   www.em-media.org.uk
➢ Screen East   www.screeneast.co.uk
➢ Northern Film And Media   www.northernmedia.org
➢ North West Vision And Media www.northwestvision.co.uk
➢ Screen West Midlands   www.screenwm.co.uk
➢ South West Screen   www.swscreen.co.uk
➢ CinemaNX – Isle of Man: www.cinemanx.com

GERMANY
The Federal Film Fund was launched in 2007 and has been a success. German producers with company headquarters in Germany, plus foreign companies with a registered office or a subsidiary in Germany, can apply for the Federal Film Fund/DFFF's non-repayable grant on part of the German expenditures for theatrical features. The regional funds are also very important film funding sources. www.location-germany.de
"Inglorious Basterds" accessed German funding:
• $450,000 - MDM – regional fund
• $900,000 - Medienboard Berlin-Brandenburg – regional fund
• $10m - German Federal Film Fund/DFFF
What the Program Provides?
German Federal Film Fund: The film producer can receive a grant, 20% for every euro of production cost spent in Germany, up to a maximum

of 80% of a film's total production costs. A minimum of 25% of those costs must be spent in Germany. A €4m cap per film can be increased to €10m if the costs spent in Germany amounts to at least 35% of a film's total production costs, or if two-thirds of the points of the cultural test are attained. Total production cost of at least $1.5m

How Does Producer Access the Money?
75% of the film's financing must be in place when making an application for the fund and has not started shooting yet.

Is the Money Upfront or Back–End?
Grant is received back-end after production is completed.

Is There a Cultural or Other Requirement?
Yes

Can Other Territories Incentives Also Be Used In Conjunction?
Yes - in that, it works well with other German regional funds, but it is more difficult with other international incentives.

Producer's Likes & Dislikes.

Likes:
Easy and it works and it is a grant.

Dislikes:
Need to have a German distributor signed for a theatrical release.

Films That Have Used the Program.
"Inglorious Basterds"

Contact Information
Christine Berg, project manager, DFFF
Web: www.ffa.de/dfff

German Regional Funds
These funds are an important part of the German film incentive program and often go in tandem with the German Federal Film Fund and can provide valuable funding. They focus on international co-productions and local German partners and have clear guidelines on what needs to be spent in the region to get these funds.

➢ Filmstiftung NRW
➢ Nordmedia
➢ Medienboard Berlin-Brandenburg
➢ Filmforderung Hamburg Schleswig-Holstein
➢ FFF Bayern
➢ MFG Filmforderung
➢ MDM Mitteldeutsche Medienforderung

IRELAND

Section 481 has been active in some form since 1987. It is a straight forward program that pays out up to 28% of qualifying expenditure on the first day of principal photography or when financing is completed. Ardmore Studios is Ireland's most well-known facility. It is small relative to the major UK/European studios.

What the Program Provides?

Section 481 provides up to 28% of qualifying expenditures and is capped at 80% of the film's budget. Can pay this incentive on first day of production if all financing in place.

How Does Producer Access the Money?

Need to partner with an Irish producer who submits the application.

Is the Money Upfront or Back–End?

Once film financing is closed the incentive can be received.

Is There a Cultural or Other Requirement?

Yes – cultural test is loose but also need an Irish partner.

Can Other Territories Incentives Also Be Used In Conjunction?

Incentive applies only to spend in Ireland, but Ireland is part of EU convention and has numerous international co-production treaties.

Producer's Likes & Dislikes.

Likes:

Money is upfront.

Covers TV series also.

Films That Have Used the Program.

"The Escapist"

Contact Information

Naoise Barry, Film Commissioner, Irish Film Board

Web: www.irishfilmboard.ie

AUSTRALIA

Australia's relatively new 40% producer incentive (2007) makes Australia attractive to the country's independent filmmakers. The government wants the incentive to be the method of production finance in Australia, rather than the direct subsidy system that also exists. However, Aussie producers are not used to working with banks and financiers.

What the Program Provides?

Two Parts:

- *40% Producer Offset* – 40% of qualifying Australian production costs on eligible Australian films and official co-productions providing each film over A$ 1m.
- *15% Post/Location Offset (PDV)* – 15% of qualifying costs of films of any nationality for post or location work with cost minimums in place.

How Does Producer Access the Money?

Film should be completed, then apply to obtain certificate and submit to tax authorities.

Is the Money Upfront or Back–End?

Back-end

Is There a Cultural or Other Requirement?

For the 40% -yes - need to pass Australia significant content ruling production. If co-production then already eligible. For the 15% - no test.

Can Other Territories Incentives Also Be Used In Conjunction?

Yes, for official co-productions.

Producer's Likes & Dislikes.

Likes:

40% is very attractive.

Dislikes:

Just make sure you understand the fine print.

Films That Have Used the Program.

"Australia"

Contact Information

Alex Sangston, head of co-production/producer offset, Screen Australia

Web: www.screenaustralia.gov.au/produceroffset

Web: www.arts.gov.au/film/australianscreenproductionincentive

NEW ZEALAND

This country is humming with film success, whether it be "Lord of the Rings", "The Hobbit", "Avatar", etc. The LBSPG and the PDVG are there to attract international production and are triggered when a certain level of New Zealand expenditure is reached, namely $1.1m and $2.2m respectively. Producers can apply for one or the other. The incentives are easy and clear.

What the Program Provides?

Two major parts:

- *Screen Production Incentive Fund (PDVG)* - 40% return of qualifying expenditures for NZ producers of a NZ film and also official co-productions (minimum costs are $3m).
- *Large Budget Grant (LBSPG)/Post Grant (PDVG)* - 15% return of qualifying costs of films of any nationality using NZ as a location or for post.

How Does Producer Access the Money?

Application made once production is completed.

Is the Money Upfront or Back–End?

Back-end for the 40%. The 15% is an upfront grant.

Is There a Cultural or Other Requirement?

For the 40% - yes - but if co-production then eligible. For the 15% - no.

Can Other Territories Incentives Also Be Used In Conjunction?

Yes

Producer's Likes & Dislikes.

Likes:

40% provides real equity and it works.

15% is a grant so it is like cash and there is no real wait.

Dislikes:

For the 40% - the minimum qualifying costs threshold.

Films That Have Used the Program.

40% - "Under the Mountain"

15% - "Avatar", " Jumper"

Contact Information

Sarah Cull, head of business affairs, New Zealand Film Commission

Web: www.nzfilm.co.nz

OTHER COUNTRIES WITH SIGNIFICANT FILM INCENTIVE PROGRAMS ARE:

- ➢ FRANCE   www.filmfrance.net
- ➢ ITALY   www.ape-italy.com
- ➢ SPAIN   www.mcu.es/cine
- ➢ MALTA   www.mfc.com.mt
- ➢ BELGIUM   www.vaf.be

- LUXEMBOURG   www.filmfund.lu
- ICELAND   www.filminiceland.com
- HUNGARY   www.filminhungary.com
- SOUTH AFRICA   www.thedfi.gov.za
- SOUTH KOREA   www.koreanfilm.or.kr
- SINGAPORE   www.mda.gov.sg
- TAIWAN   www.taipeifilmcommission.org
- BRAZIL   www.abrafic.org
- CAYMAN ISLANDS   www.cifilm.ky
- FIJI   www.fijiaudiovisual.com
- ISRAEL   www.filmfund.org.il/
- MEXICO   www.comefilm.gob.mx
- HOLLAND   www.filmfund.nl

FILM FINANCE GLOSSARY

Above-the-Line Costs - The ABL is an important part of the top sheet of a budget. ABL comprises the creative elements, story rights and screenplay, executive producer and producer, direction, principal cast, as well as sundry costs.

Adjusted Gross Deal - Adjusted gross deal is a distribution agreement where the distributor deducts from gross receipts the costs of co-operative advertising and other items and then divides the balance, the adjusted gross, with the producer.

Ancillary Rights - These are rights which may be capable of exploitation that come as a result of the production of a film, as distinct from the exploitation of the film itself. They include merchandising rights, television spin-off rights, sequel, prequel and remake rights, book publishing rights, computer game rights, soundtrack album rights, and the music publishing rights in the score.

Below-the-Line Costs - The top sheet of a budget is divided into sections. First section deals with above-the-line costs. Then production, editing, etc. are the below-the-line costs. Total budget, comprises the above-the-line costs, the below-the-line costs, the completion guarantee fee, the contingency and the fringes.

Cash Flow - The cash flow is usually set out in a schedule based on the budget and shows the money sums, over time, required for the production of the film. The cash flow will also show the source of funds.

Chain of Title - The route by which the producer's right to use copyright material may be traced from the author to the producer through a `chain' of assignments and transfers.

Co-Operative Advertising - Advertising, the cost of which is shared between the distributor and exhibitors.

Co-Production Treaty - An agreement between countries which may permit films made in or with resources from both countries to benefit from soft money/subsidies available from both countries.

Completion Guarantee - An agreement under which a completion guarantor guarantees to the financiers of a film, or a distributor who has advanced money prior to delivery, that the film will be completed and delivered by a given date to its principal distributors in accordance with the relevant distribution agreements (agreed script/agreed actors, etc.).

Completion Guarantor - A company which is in the business of providing completion guarantees for a film and its financiers.

Contingency - An amount added to the budget of a film to cover unforeseen circumstances, usually 10% of the budgeted cost, excluding the completion guarantee fee.

Copyright Search - A search in the US Copyright Office to see if any interest in the film has been registered.

Costs Off The Top - A distribution agreement where distribution expenses are deducted from gross receipts. The balance is then divided between the distributor and the producer in agreed shares.

Cross Collateralization - The assigning of film revenues derived from one source, whether a territory or a form of exploitation, towards the recoupment of an advance, irrespective of revenues arising from another territory or form of exploitation all falling within the same grant to a sales agent. Cross-collateralized can mean the revenues earned from several markets (and/or multi films) are pooled. For example, say your film made $100,000 in France and lost $100,000 in Italy. If those territories were cross-collateralized, and the producer was entitled to a percentage of the net revenue, you would get nothing. Similarly, if the territories were not cross-collateralized, producer would get the % of the French revenues and the distributor would absorb the loss incurred in Italy. In a multi-territory or multi-film distribution agreement, cross-collateralization is usually prohibited, meaning that each picture must stand on its own and the distributor may not offset gains and losses from different territories or films.

Deferment - A sum payable to a writer, actor, director, producer or similar connected with a film out of revenues derived from the exploitation of the film, but after the deduction of distribution fees and expenses and, usually, after the financiers and the completion guarantor have recovered all of the sums they have advanced towards the cost of production and delivery of the film.

Distribution Agreement - An agreement under which rights to exploit a film in one or more media is granted. The distributor grants rights as principal, not as agent. The agreement will provide either for a lump sum payment by the distributor or for a sharing of revenues.

Distributor - A party which organizes film distribution under a distribution agreement.

Domestic Rights - The rights to distribute a film in North America.

Errors & Omissions (E&O) Insurance - Insurance against claims arising out of infringements of copyright, defamation and unauthorized use of names, trade names, trademarks or characters.

Favored Nation Terms - The most favorable terms accorded to any party to a transaction, including that no one will get any better terms or if any improved terms are granted to a third party then the `favored nation' will be treated equally.

Final Cut - The final say on the editing of a film.

Foreign Rights - The converse of domestic rights, they are the rights to distribute a film outside America.

Four Walling - The practice where a producer rents the cinema and all the seats for all the shows for a week (usually at a discount) and then shows their own film and collects the box office.

Free Television - A television broadcast intended for reception by the public where no charge is made to the consumer.

Gap Financing - A specialty lending arrangement, whereby, a bank will lend the difference between production finance raised and the minimum expected from sales by a reputable sales agent. Usually this does not exceed ten to fifteen percent of the budget of a film.

Holdback - A period of time during which a particular form of exploitation is not allowed - eg. From theatrical release to DVD release.

Minimum Guarantee - The minimum sum a distributor guarantees will be payable to a producer as a result of the distributor's distribution of the film. The guaranteed sum may be payable at the beginning of the distribution period, as an advance against the producer's share of the proceeds of distribution.

Negative Pick-Up - A distribution agreement where the advance is payable only on delivery of the finished film to the distributor.

NTSC - National Television System - the code system used in the USA and Japan by which color television pictures are distributed or transmitted using 525 lines.

Off-Balance Sheet Finance - An arrangement under which a loan is made to a company without the debt appearing on the investor's balance sheet and affecting its gearing ratio.

Option - In film, an option is a right that can be exercised during a specific period for a specific sum to acquire certain rights.

Overages - Distribution revenues payable to the producer after the advance or minimum guarantee has been recouped.

P & A Commitment - A contractual obligation imposed on a distributor to spend specified minimum sums on prints and advertising to support the initial theatrical release of a film.

Packaging - The provision, usually by a talent agency, of a package of individuals to work on a film. The package might consider any one or more of the director, screenplay writer, stars and members of the supporting cast.

PAL - Phase Alternative Line - the code system by which color television pictures are distributed or transmitted using 625 lines. PAL is also used in an increasing number of countries in Europe.

Pay or Play - A commitment to pay a director or performer made before production commences, and sometimes before all the finance has become unconditional, regardless of whether his or her services are used.

Pay Television - Television programming (other than basic cable) for which the consumer has to pay.

Points - Shares of back-end or net profits in a film are measured in percentage points. To have points in a film means to have a share of the net profits.

Pre-Sale - A license or distribution agreement entered into before a film has been completed. The advance, minimum guarantee or license fee payable under the pre-sale may form part of the finance package for the film.

Private Investor or Angel - An individual, often having little direct connection with the film industry, who invests his own money in a film.

Producer's Share of Net Profits - Net profits are what is left of revenues from the exploitation of the film after distribution fees and expenses, repayment of any loans and investments raised to finance production, repayment of any sums extended by the completion guarantor and the payment of any deferments. Net profits are normally divided between the investors and the producer. The producer's share is usually between 40-60% of the net profits, out of which the producer may have to pay the profit entitlements (points) of various individuals and others who have contributed towards the film.

Recoupment Order - The order in which investors and financiers are repaid their loans and investments (and interest).

Residual - A sum of money, payable under a union, guild or individual agreement, to a performer, musician, writer, composer, director or producer.

SAG - Screen Actors Guild

Sales Agent - An agent appointed by the producer to act as agent for the sale of the film. See also distributor.

Tax Shelter - A relief, allowance, deduction or credit for taxation purposes which has the effect of eliminating, reducing, or deferring, a liability of tax.

Television Rights - The collective expression includes a number of different forms of television, such as free and pay television and terrestrial and satellite television. When granting television rights, care should be taken to be specific as to the rights granted if revenues are to be maximized.

Theatrical Rights - The rights to exhibit the film in cinemas and other places of public viewing to which the general public is admitted and for which an admission charge in money or money's worth is made.

Window - A period during which a particular form of exploitation of a film may take place, for example, a free television window.

18 THINGS YOU SHOULD KNOW ABOUT FILM FINANCING:
1) WHAT IS IT YOU ARE SELLING? - FILM PACKAGE
2) HOW MUCH AND WHY?
3) KNOW HOW TO GET MONEY BACK!
4) WHAT DO THEY GET?
5) ARE YOU PREPARED? – all your materials
6) KNOW YOUR PITCH.
7) SELL YOURSELF.
8) KNOW YOUR TIME LINE.
9) HAVE A CLEAR LEGAL STRUCTURE.
10) KNOW YOUR POTENTIAL INVESTOR.
11) BE PREPARED TO NEGOTIATE
12) HAVE AN ENTERTAINMENT LAWYER READY.
13) UNDERSTAND THE MANY FILMFUNDING OPTIONS.
14) TENACITY & PERSEVERANCE
15) DO NOT BS & BE POLITE & PROFESSIONAL.
16) STEVEN SPIELBERG YOU ARE NOT!
17) FINANCING TAKES TIME.
18) MONEY IS NOT THERE UNTIL YOU ARE SPENDING IT.

****

CREATIVE/PRODUCING

HIGHLIGHTS OF THIS CHAPTER...

PRODUCER - OR NOT TO BE A PRODUCER

GUIDELINES FOR PRODUCER SUCCESS

THINGS A PRODUCER SHOULD KNOW

ACTORS, AGENTS, AND AGENCIES

TEN THINGS THAT HOLLYWOOD
DOESN'T WANT YOU TO KNOW

SCRIPTS & WRITERS

CREATIVE/PRODUCING
"So You Want To Be In The Movies?"

"No one goes out to make a bad movie they just happen!"
Best quote I have ever heard from a studio executive.

The world of studios and the world of independents is night and day. I have worked in both worlds and that statement is so true. Therefore, let's continue in that mode and take a look at the following:

HOLLYWOOD - THE THREE BIG LIES
There is a certain mystic and aura around the film industry and Hollywood in particular. Let me help remove some of the BS that is perpetuated by the industry.

Lie #1 - Filmmaking is an art form – wrong!
How nice to think of it as an art form and in some ways it is; but, to the film industry making films is a business. There is a reason it is called the "film business". Why, because to make movies is big business that demands big money – cash! Once the money is paid out, then we need to get it back and hopefully make a profit. This is business – do not think otherwise.

Lie #2 – Film industry is all about producing films - wrong!
The film industry is really a huge marketing machine that spends more on marketing a film than on making a film. The huge budget for marketing a film or what is called the P & A (Prints and Advertising), covers all the TV/radio/newspaper/magazine spending, plus all the posters and trailers. This advertising goes on all around the world. The advertising/marketing starts as the film is about to be released into cinemas, then continues through DVD release, then into TV release, etc. – the marketing of a film cycle. The marketing focus is always on who is in the movie and what the film budget is.

Remember a film has absolutely no value unless someone buys it! So a film becomes a movie when it goes into a cinema or into a DVD release. Marketing pushes the product in order for the general public to pay to see it. In each step of the distribution cycle, theatrical-DVD-TV-ancillary, marketing is designed to extract dollars from the public who pay to see the film.

Lie #3 – The Budget!

Normally any company that makes a product for resale will never tell anyone how much the item cost to make – not so in the film industry. Here the budget figure of the film is proudly told to the general public with much publicity and fanfare. It is a marketing exercise. Guess what? It does not matter where the budget of a film is - $200m or just $5m you still pay your $9 or so to get into the cinema! Do you think the film industry really tells you the truth? Often budgets of studio films are highly inflated and seem to be marketed to ensure a "wow" factor - eg. Avatar: $200m plus. Marketing...marketing...marketing!

INDEPENDENTS VS STUDIOS

The film industry is clearly split into two significant camps – one, the "studios" and two, the "independents". This book is focused on the independent film business; however, we must understand the industry as a whole.

"The Studios" or "The Majors" are terms specifically related to the six large film companies that dominate the film industry. The six studios are:

➢ 20th Century Fox
➢ Paramount
➢ Sony Pictures
➢ Columbia Pictures
➢ Disney
➢ Universal

All six are located in the USA around Los Angeles, California. These studios (have large studio lots with sound stages – hence term "studios") operate as fully self-contained units in the film industry. They develop, finance, produce, sell, market and distribute their own films, both in the US and internationally. These studios control all the rights to the films they produce. The majors are the dominant force in the film industry and control the market for large budget films being seen on the cinema screens across the world.

An "independent" can be termed anything that is not a studio. Usually the term relates to films whose budget is significantly below that of a studio. If a studio budget is typically at an average of $60m (rising to hundreds of millions) with a prints and advertising budget of another $30m, then an independent film is often considerably lower in production cost than a studio film. Therefore, an independent film is a film that is not developed or produced by a film studio or even distributed by a studio - but is produced and sold independently and a studio has nothing to do with the film whatsoever.

This definition has, over the recent years, slightly blurred as the studios have actively made efforts to spread the commercial risk of their films with other studios or film partners around the world; plus, the studios have actively converted film companies that were thought of as independents and have now been acquired by studios – such as New Line, Working Title and Miramax (aka "mini-majors"). These movements are continuing today and represent a fluid approach by the studios to help their commercial risk strategy of film producing, developing and distributing.

To help clarify for the purposes of this book, an "independent film" relates to the fact that the film has been financed (in large part anyway), produced, marketed and distributed outside the studio system.

So in essence there three types of film made:
- Studio films (six studios)
- Independent studio films (studio independent divisions – Fox Searchlight/New Line – smaller budgets – not really independent, but have an independent feel!)
- Independent films (made for $5k upwards)

However, the definition is fluid and things get a bit murkier when you look at say George Lucas and Star Wars. He is a real independent filmmaker, but Fox funds the film and distributes it – therefore, it is a studio film.

FIVE STAGES OF FILMMAKING:

- ❖ **Development** - The script is written for a feature film.
- ❖ **Pre-Production** - Preparations are made for the shoot in which cast and crew are hired, locations are selected, and sets are built, etc.
- ❖ **Production** – The film is created and shot over a period of weeks.
- ❖ **Post-Production** - The film is edited; music tracks (and songs) are composed, performed and recorded; sound effects are designed and recorded; and any other computer graphic 'visual' effects are digitally added, and the film is fully completed.
- ❖ **Marketing, Sales and Distribution** - The film is marketed, screened for potential buyers (distributors), is picked up by a distributor and reaches its theater and/or DVD & TV audience.

Note: Since the introduction of digital technology, the means of production have become much more available, cheaper and easier. Filmmakers can shoot and edit a movie, create and edit the sound and music, and mix the final cut on a home computer. However, while the means of production may be easier, financing, distribution, and marketing remain difficult to accomplish outside the traditional system. Most independent filmmakers rely on film festivals to get their films noticed and sold for distribution; but, the internet has allowed for relatively inexpensive distribution of independent films. Many filmmakers post their films online for critique and recognition. Although there is little profitability in this, a filmmaker can still gain exposure via the web and this can lead to new and exciting opportunities for revenue sources.

PRODUCTION PROCESS -PRE/PROD/POST

With a great script in hand and financing in place the adventure begins – how to make a film. As I have said, the purpose of my book is not to include a "how to shoot a low budget independent feature film" – many other titles do a great job in informing filmmakers how to shoot and finish a film. Therefore, I will not delve into that world even though I have spent many, many hours in producing, being on set, and being involved in the production process, both in TV (MASH) and in my own feature films (refer to IMDB). However, I will summarize some of the more important functions and areas relating to the production process that I deem important.

Scheduling & Budgeting -These two items go hand in hand and it is reasonable to assume that as this is a low budget film a producer has a fixed amount of film financing to complete the film. Scheduling a film involves doing a script breakdown that identifies what scenes from the script can be shot together in the same day, scheduling actors to work on consecutive days, etc. In other words, work out the most efficient and cost effective way of shooting the film. The actual budget may only allow a certain number of shooting days so a production manager has to be creative - fit so much into a tight budget. This process is detailed and requires an experienced production manager to effectively pull the schedule and the final budget together – and hopefully is within the budget available, otherwise the fun begins and all sorts of things need to be adjusted to fit available production funding.

If your cast is union, the pay cannot be deferred (unless classified as a short or student film). However, the union, SAG (Screen Actors Guild), will allow certain films to qualify under a SAG Indie Program that will assist the producer in this area. Always check with SAG (www.sagindie.org) on what qualifies for what relief.

- *Ultra-Low Budget* – If the film budget is under $200,000, then the union allows a mix of union and non-union actors. A $100 daily flat rate is applicable.

- *Modified Low Budget* – If the film budget is under $625,000 (up to $937,500) actors are paid $268 per day and all actors have to be union.

- *Low Budget* - If the film budget is under $2.5m actors are paid $504 per day and all actors have to be union.

ATL / BTL - A film budget is split between Above-the-Line (ATL) items and Below-the-Line (BTL) items.

The ATL items usually relate to the talent and the creative elements plus producers. Therefore, the actors, director, writers and producers are included in this category. Above-the-line expenditures are those that are negotiated or spent before filming begins. These costs can include rights for the material on which the screenplay is based and the salaries for the screenwriter, producer, actors, director, and assistants to director.

The BTL includes those that actually make the film – the crew, department heads and all the various functions required to make the film. Below-the-line costs include the salaries of the non-starring cast members and the technical crew, as well as costs of technical equipment, travel, filming location, and catering costs, etc.

Locations - The script will identify different locations where scenes take place. Therefore, it is necessary to try, in a cost effective manner, to find such locations. A location scout can do this or you can do it yourself. Once found the location manager manages those locations for the shoot. There are many aspects to locations that must be addressed as it is not usually a smart thing to start shooting on location without first thoroughly checking out the location for such things as film permits, parking restrictions, traffic, etc.

Storyboarding - Storyboards are graphic organizers such as a series of illustrations or images displayed in sequence for the purpose of pre-visualizing a film. A film storyboard is essentially a large comic strip of the film produced before the film starts production to help the director visualize the story/scenes.

Crew - Every film production needs crew. A film crew is a group of people hired by a production company for the purpose of producing a film. The crew is divided into different departments, each of which specializes in a specific aspect of the film production process which include art, sets, props, construction, scenic, greens, wardrobe/ costume, hair/ makeup, camera, sound, grip, electric, transportation, editorial, visual effects, music. It is not unusual for low budget films not to deal with unions for crew positions. IATSE and Teamsters are very strict.

Talent - *"When an actor comes to me and wants to discuss his character, I say, 'It's in the script.' If he says, 'But what's my motivation?' I say, 'Your salary.'"*   ---- *Alfred Hitchcock*

A script only comes to life with actors; or in some cases, dies a slow death because the actors are terrible! How does one find actors for a low budget independent feature film? It is likely Brad Pitt and Julia Roberts will be unavailable so we must aim a bit lower.

It is important to realize that unless your script is just unbelievable it is not probable you will get any real named actors. But, if you are lucky you may get a B-rated actor to help both in quality and in marketability of your project. If you live in Los Angeles and you network, it could happen that a friend knows a friend, who knows an actor, who is great friends with a B-actor and is available to read your script and could conceivably want to do your film.

Networking in LA works and works well. I remember when my good writer/director friend had a good friend who was very close to Dolph Lundgren. At the time in the early 90's he was a marketable action star for independent films. Because of that connection we had meetings with Dolph (and agent plus lawyer) and came really close to a multi–million dollar deal on a film project entitled "Le Tigre".

Casting is very important. There are lots of actors (or wannabes) all over the planet. Some are really good, but most are really bad. Most talent (including directors and producers, writers, etc.) have their credits on IMDB (www.imdb.com). Actors can be found at acting classes, friends, calling agents/managers, placing advertisements in say "Backstage" or at your local coffee shop! The process of actor selection is usually a long tedious one, but at the end your selection can mean the difference between a good film and a pitiful film.

Once actors are selected, written agreements must be prepared and signed. If using a SAG (Screen Actors Guild) or AFTRA actor then all contracts fall under their rules. For independent film, there are SAG agreements to cover that level of budget. If actors are non-union use a deal memo at first, then follow up with long form agreement later. These terms (deal memo & long form) are basic industry terms that are used in many areas of the film business.

Non-union actor contractual points that will cover both parties are:
➤ Character to be played - the role.
➤ Number of shooting days and rehearsal days.
➤ Acting fee – including any deferments and net profit points.
➤ Per diem and other benefits.
➤ Post-production sound days.
➤ Credit billing.

Shooting/Production/Directing - As I have said before, this book is not about how to shoot a film. But, here are some tips I have learned over many years that during production you need to be aware of:
➤ Check the weather.

- Rehearse, rehearse, rehearse – helps later.
- On location, check for surrounding noise.
- Test the camera and make sure it works. Have extra memory chips.
- Make sure the batteries are working (for all devices especially sound) and have back up batteries.
- Have backup locations – just in case.
- Give good driving instructions for locations.
- Cell phones don't work everywhere!
- Make sure there is plenty of parking.
- Make sure all permits are obtained and up to date.
- Make sure you have food and drink for lunch break.

Post-Production – editing/music/special effects/credits/titles - Is it amazing what today's computers, and the associated editing software, can do for filmmaking? One should say – what they cannot do. The days of splicing 35mm negative are long, long gone. Now you can edit images, sound, create effects, do titles, etc., all in the comfort of your own home.

These are some of the considerations regarding editing:
- Choose the best take - goes without saying!
- Beware of the pacing – editing can slow or speed up the film story.
- Match shots - moving shots with moving shots and static with static.
- Continuity – watch for shots of same scene from different takes that have continuity problems.
- Watch your order of shots and scenes – ensure integrity of a scene is maintained and not changed by editing.
- Watch length of scenes – too long a scene(s) can really slow down the story.

The best film magazines and information publications:
- Daily Variety
- Hollywood Reporter
- Backstage
- Video Maker
- Moviemaker magazine
- Student Filmmakers magazine
- Hollywood Creative Directory

➢ Screen International
➢ DV magazine
➢ American Cinematographer

In addition to the above, the internet has provided a huge number of film communities and film forums that create resources for filmmakers to exchange and transfer information and experiences. - eg. "Meetup" groups.

PRODUCER - OR NOT TO BE A PRODUCER!

Who are these people?

Executive Producer: As many titles are - this one is often abused. In truth an Executive Producer is the person who is responsible to make the whole film project happen. This usually entails ensuring the film package (script, director and lead talent) is in place and that the film is fully financed and ,where possible, some form of domestic and/or foreign distribution is in place (before, during or after completion). The Executive Producer can also oversee the production, post and distribution of the film.

Producer: This is the person who has ultimate responsibility to "produce" the film – from inception/script to screen. The Producer is the lead person on all matters regarding the pre-production, production, post-production and delivery of the film. In addition, the Producer has responsibility for obtaining and repaying the film funding and also controls the copyright of the film.

Line Producer: Also known as the Production Manager, the Line Producer has extensive production experience and is the main production person of the film. He ensures the film is produced in accordance with the script and budget.

Associate Producer: This title is also abused often in the film industry. Sometimes it is a title given for services rendered and not necessarily to do with production - more an honorary title. Other times the Associate Producer can be a provider to the film of special services such as the original owner of the script.

Co-Producer: The producing responsibilities for the film are split. Each is a Co-Producer.

WHAT A PRODUCER DOES

A producer must shepherd the film project through the complete cycle - from inception, development, financing, production through marketing and distribution. Relationships must be maintained and nurtured with investors, crew, talent, agents, banks, marketers, lawyers, distributors and your own producing team – a true balancing act!

In reality producers tend to come as two types – firstly, there is the producer-dealmaker and then, there is the producer-filmmaker. Both are producers, but they have different orientations to the job. One is more about negotiating and finding the right deals - the second is more the filmmaker/the production person/the maker of films. To be a truly effective producer you need to be a hybrid of both types.

A good producer should have the following traits:

➤ *Story/Script* – ability to identify and work the story and the script.
➤ *Contacts* – access to useful film industry contacts.
➤ *Master Salesperson* – ability to sell ice to the eskimos and get financing.
➤ *Negotiator* – ability to be an effective dealmaker.
➤ *Diplomat/Dictator* – ability to handle people and get the best out of them.
➤ *Persistence and Never Say Die* – have a positive attitude and great energy.
➤ *Multi-Tasker Extraordinaire* – be able to handle many tasks and problems and find equitable solutions.
➤ *Organizer* – strategy, planning and organization abilities to get the job done on time and on budget.

Producers must look to the film's potential earnings and what elements may affect such earnings whether it is a big budget film or a low budget independent film. Some of the elements that can effect revenue potential can be split into two camps for discussion; namely, distribution/marketing factors and secondly, story/production factors.

Distribution/Marketing Factors:
- The season in which the film is released
- The awareness, interest and effectiveness of the marketing campaign to the target audience
- Target audience saturation density – reach and frequency
- The theatrical release pattern
- Critical reviews
- Other films released in the same time frame

Story/Production Factors:
- Effect of film's genre
- Running time of film
- Use of star actor power or not
- Film's rating
- Budget/cost to potential earnings

GUIDELINES FOR PRODUCER SUCCESS

The following principles are applicable to all successful producers:

The Story: The essence of any film is the story, the concept, the idea. A producer must search and find a quality story and develop it until satisfied. The process of script development is a very important aspect of the movie process and is often the most time intensive, where creative thoughts constantly are evolving towards a final product.

Development: The process of taking an idea and writing a script then re-writing and editing can be a long and sometimes expensive process. Producers often find investors to help finance this area of the film process and careful negotiations need to be made regarding repayment and profit sharing.

Target Audience: A producer, based on the story and genre of the film, should have a clear idea of specific target audiences. Such audiences need to be defined and the producer should clearly understand who the audience is, their demographic, geographic and economic profiles. This should also include the film's appeal to international audiences. A clear and concise view on who your film appeals to and the target audience is a must in both selling the film to investors and to potential distributors.

Financing: Production financing is a very difficult task and a major section of this book covers film financing. To understand all the various avenues available to producers for financing is an important requirement of a film producer. Obviously, budget levels and locations will dictate which financing strategy to focus on. Regarding previously acquired development money it is not unusual that development investors are paid out from the new incoming production investors.

Negotiating/Entertainment Law: Producers must be business orientated, not just creative. Negotiating all forms of deals and contracts come with the territory of film producer. Knowing and understanding fundamental principles of contract law, entertainment law and the usual film industry standard terms and conditions will benefit the production. The art of negotiation is also something that is of benefit. Being able to talk the film industry lingo is a real benefit and will open doors, rather than have them slammed on you for being ignorant of the industry you purport to be in.

Talent: The comments made in the section above definitely apply when dealing with talent and the whole process of approaching agents and finalizing with lawyers to obtain the talent's services. Deal making meetings with the agents, manager and attorneys can be daunting but preparation, planning and industry research will help in the process.

Distribution: Another area where a producer must research and understand the many avenues of distribution available to independent films. Such understanding will not only include the US and Canadian markets, but, also the many countries that are the international market. A clear understanding of the rights involved in licensing a film is a must – theatrical, DVD, TV and ancillary, plus all the windows associated with those rights.

Team Leader: Producing a film whether big budget or low budget requires many skills. One of these skills is being a team leader and having the ability to manage many different situations and many different personality types as a film moves through the process from inception to screen – a daunting task.

10 THINGS A PRODUCER SHOULD KNOW:
1) NO STORY - NO FILM!
2) UNDERSTAND "THE PACKAGE" & FILM GENRE
3) UNDERSTAND THE FILMMAKING PROCESS
4) UNDERSTAND FILM FINANCING & BUSINESS PLANS
5) UNDERSTAND MARKETING, PUBLICITY AND PROMOTION
6) UNDERSTAND THE INTERNET
7) FOREIGN IS VERY IMPORTANT
8) UNDERSTAND FOREIGN SALES AGENTS
9) DESPERATION IS NOT A GOOD THING
10) LEARN TO SAY NO

FIRST FILM PROJECT – Now what?

I have often been asked what kind of film script should a - "new to the business" producer/writer, make for their first film project. The answer is, a project that takes between 4 to 6 good looking teenagers, put them in a house and slaughter them one at a time – chop them up in creative ways, set it at night and make it full of tension and suspense. That is a guaranteed hit around the world! Why?

➢ Horror sells all over the world.
➢ You do not need named actors to help sell film.
➢ A house is the only location so it is cheap to shoot.
➢ Shoot at night, so you hide potential camera/lighting issues.
➢ Everyone loves looking at good looking people.
➢ Everyone loves to be scared.
➢ You can create great marketing materials that are provocative and compelling.

The key to writing a good low budget script is creativity and originality. With such a low, low budget, a script must carry the film from start to finish - the creative element will keep the audience guessing and interested in the development of the story.

LET'S TALK GENRES!

What is genre and why is it important in the film world? A genre is a specific category that has its own particular characterizations, style or form of content. Film genres will include action, family, sci-fi, drama, horror, romantic comedy, comedy, fantasy, western, thriller, musical, animation, etc.

It is usual that a film project fall into a genre as this will help describe the film to an audience or a buyer or film executive. Certain genres at certain times become the flavor of the month. During the independent video boom, erotic thrillers were in major demand for a period, as were the action genre films. Then for a time horror was the hot genre. Certainly, in recent times the comic book action hero genre has been popular. Your story will fall into a genre. Some genres are better suited for international audiences than others. For instance, action and horror movies tend to be universal; however, comedies and romantic comedies can be less successful due to cultural differences. This is especially so when the film is a low budget independent film with no recognizable named actors – not every film can have Julia Roberts to ensure it is an international success!

FILM OR DIGITAL? - THAT IS THE QUESTION

In the boom days of the independent filmmaker - ie. In the 1990s, film was the preferred method – the only real method. The choice was whether to go super 8 or 16mm or the top of the line 35mm. The traditional formats are still used, but the 35mm film stock remains the accepted method for mainstream studio and higher budgeted films. Certainly, if the film is meant for the cinema it is still the 35mm print that is the format of choice.

The world of digital has opened up a new world for filmmakers, especially the new independent filmmaker who is out to make a name for themselves and create a film for little cash outlay yet still get acceptable results. Digital 24p HD camcorder is here and provides a look of film without the expense of film stock, lab and printing costs, and telecine costs. The HD digital cameras have now come into a price range that is accessible to the general public. Anyone now can shoot a film.

Advantages of the digital HD camcorder in summary are:
➢ Tapes or memory chips are cheaper than film.
➢ No processing/developing costs.
➢ Camcorder is smaller, lighter and more maneuverable than film cameras.
➢ Reloading is kept to minimum.
➢ Image is seen instantly.
➢ Digital sound can be excellent.
➢ Editing systems are easy to use.

Note: Be careful when using camcorders for lighting, contrast and sound. These three areas can be of concern when delivering (for a sale) a digital-master to a foreign TV station and the master might fail QC (quality control).

SO YOU HAVE AN IDEA, STORY OR EVEN A SYNOPSIS – NOW WHAT?

You want to make a movie from your idea or story but how do you do it? What are the steps? So let's say you have put pen to paper and written the bare bones of your idea into a two or three page story synopsis. This synopsis has the basic story line, locations and a short description on the leading characters. Hopefully, the story is an interesting one with a beginning, middle and end. What now?

This story/synopsis needs to be turned into a screenplay (a properly formatted manuscript that follows industry guidelines). To do this one can write it yourself or find a writer to do it for you.

Should you wish to find a writer there are a number of ways to do that:
➢ *Access the web* – go to writers for hire sites, such as InkTip.com.
➢ *Place ad in film trade papers* – Backstage.com or Hollywood Reporter.
➢ *Read screenplay magazines* – Script Magazine or Creative Screenwriting - they will direct you to writers groups, etc.
➢ *Ask someone who knows the film business.*
➢ *Contact writers' agents* – look to Hollywood Creative Directory (Hollywood Reporter).

SCRIPTS & WRITERS

Here are some general comments about scripts:

➢ **Scripts are normally structured into three acts** - the beginning, the middle and the end. Not rocket science - but, amazing how many scripts do not have that structure!

➢ **Create conflict and a story arc** - Conflict moves the story along and gives it substance. Therefore, avoid predictability. Try to be original. Always maintain believability. Have the story go somewhere that is interesting.

➢ **Make sure it grabs the reader in first 10 pages** - otherwise you will lose them.

➢ **Characters** - The characters you create should be real and well-rounded. Try to make the audience care about at least one of the main characters.

➢ **Read a great script** - like "Seven" to help know what a good script feels like and also read one or more good books on screen writing.

➢ **Come up with a marketable title** - eg. "The reckless banana - a love story" - just joking!

➢ **Have other screenwriters read your work** - Obtain constructive criticism.

➢ **An independent script for a 90 minute feature film is about 105 pages** - give or take.

➢ **Use an industry acknowledged screen writing software** - eg. Final Draft

➢ **Always register your screenplay** - The Writers Guild of America has an online registration site - www.wgaregistry.org and click online registration service.

HOW TO GET A SCRIPT

There are basically only three ways to get a good script. Without a good script you have no hope of ever making a good film – makes sense? The old computer saying – garbage in garbage out!

1) Write your own.
2) Option a script from someone else.
3) Hire a writer to write a script for you.

Writing your own script

No simple task and demands time and a great deal of effort and technical ability in terms of understanding script/story structure.

The following steps might assist you in writing your own script:

➤ Short description of the story idea/concept.
➤ Come up with catchy title.
➤ Write a two to three page synopsis with brief description on characters and story arc, plus locations.
➤ Write a tagline - similar to what you see on movie posters – encapsulate the essence of the film - eg. The film "Alien" - "No one can hear you scream in space".
➤ Write a treatment - 20 pages plus - full story description and flow/ character description, etc.
➤ Write the script - use an industry standard script writing software.

There are many books on script writing so talk to friends/other writers with experience, etc. and select one or two books. Extract what you feel is good for you. A writer by definition is a creative person and creativity should not be placed in a box of rules and regulations that may stifle creativity. However, certain elements of story structure and character development can be discovered by reading quality script writing books.

Remember that an average low budget independent film is approximately 90 minutes long and one page of script is translated to one minute on film; therefore, look for your script to be around 90 pages.

Certainly, once your first draft is written get someone whose opinion you value to read the script. Have them answer some focused questions:

➤ Do you like the title and genre?
➤ Does the first page intrigue you?
➤ Do the first 10 pages of the script grab you and make you want to read more?
➤ Do the characters interest you and do you care about them? Do they interact with meaning?
➤ Does the story really have a beginning, middle and end?

> Does the middle sections of the script become boring or lose its way?
> Does the script have up and downs in the story to keep you interested and not puzzled as to where the story is taking you?
> Is the dialogue real and believable?

The questions can answer many of the areas you as a writer might need to address to improve your script. Ultimately, your script will have to be presented to an industry professional to get script coverage from a company that is in a position to buy the script. Script coverage is always a scary event with any writer.

Option a script

I have optioned many scripts over my many years in the film business. Let's be clear, to option is not buying a script. It is optioning the rights of the script property to purchase, for a period of time, for an amount of money.

When a screenplay is optioned, the producer has not actually purchased the right to use the screenplay. He has simply purchased the "exclusive right" to purchase the screenplay at some point in the future. A producer would then try to put together a film package that would ultimately move into a film production mode based on the optioned script. Options are very popular in Hollywood and also with producers to work with scripts without buying them – a major cost saving advantage.

During the option period, the producer must:

1) Get the screenplay written (if the option was on a book or other work, and not a screenplay).
2) Obtain informal agreements with the director, the lead actor, and the investors.
3) Find a distributor/sales agent who can provide distribution.

Once all this is in place and the financing is in the bank the production can then pay the agreed purchase price for the script. The exclusivity of the script option allows all this process to occur without risk of the script going to a rival producer.

Film options are exclusive, usually for an initial period of 12-18 months. After the expiration date the producer no longer has an exclusive right to buy the screenplay, and the writer can option it to a different producer. Most option agreements specify the price of additional extensions (most commonly one extension, also for 12-18 months), should the producer be unable to put the movie together in the originally specified term, and choose to extend. The fee for the first option period is normally applicable to the option exercise price, while the fee for the extension (if exercised) typically is not applicable, though that is not always the case.

Option agreements cover the following:

➢ *Option price* - View this as a down payment against the purchase price. A small dollar amount is payable against a larger purchase price - say $5,000 against $35,000 purchase price.

➢ *Option period* - Length of time your option will exist - usually 12 -18 months.

➢ *Purchase price* - The purchase price is a dollar amount for the producer to buy the script.

➢ *Renewal period* - It is usual to negotiate an initial option period and also a renewal period. The initial period of 18 months can be extended another 12 months for a smaller amount of money.

➢ *Re-writes* - Ensure there is an agreement with the writer to have the writer do one or more re-writes for free or included as part of the purchase price. Be careful of WGA rules.

➢ *Profit participations* - It is normal to offer a writer a percent of net profits, 5-10% is reasonable.

Note – Obtaining an option and paying out money is a serious event. Therefore, before you do that, please ensure you feel very confident that as a producer you can put the film package together and get the financing necessary. Believe me, I have paid out money for options and due to circumstances I ran out of time under the option agreement and lost the project, lost my money and lost all the many months of time I spent on trying to put the project together – heart breaking!

Hire a writer

Can we fall into development hell? Oh yes, and I have done that, so be careful. Development hell is simply the result of the producer's idea of what a story/script should be compared to the writer's (just hired) view of the story/script. They can be very different and as such when the script is presented to the producer it can be shocking! My favorite story that happened to our company was in the 1990's in Paris where we hired a French writer and paid him a significant amount of money to write a script based on an updated story line of a film that had been previously produced and was successful some years earlier. A few months later we were given a Gothic novel written in French. That was our script and that was a real shock and learning experience!

To hire a writer you can go two ways – a WGA (Writers Guild of America) writer or not. The vast majority of independent films made never see the light of day let alone a TV screen. Similarly, with screenplays – many thousands are written, very, very few are produced.

A writer that is a member of the WGA is a writer with credentials and acknowledged skills in script writing; whereas, a non-WGA writer can be anyone with or without any experience. Naturally, a WGA writer comes under the jurisdiction of the WGA (www.wga.org) and they have minimum wage scales for the different aspects of a writer's work which includes treatment, first draft, re-write and polish depending on budget levels. Do not make the mistake of thinking that just because you hire a WGA writer the script will be just what you want and it will be a great. Remember you are in the creative zone and nothing is guaranteed – except the money you have to pay the writer.

Hiring a non-WGA writer does not mean they are not capable of delivering a good script. There are many writers who are good but as yet undiscovered – just like actors. There are a number of websites that focus on writing talent and such sites should be visited and explored. I have hired non-WGA writers and they have produced scripts we shot. On average they were paid no more than $3-5,000 for the script and re-writes – a great deal for a good shooting script.

WHAT IS A LOGLINE?

A logline is a one (or occasionally two) sentence description that boils the script down to its essential dramatic narrative in a clear and concise manner. Don't tell the story, sell the story. A logline is an important part of selling or pitching your script.

WHAT IS SCRIPT COVERAGE?

Many companies in the film business receive hundreds of scripts from many sources. These companies usually send the scripts to be read and evaluated - "covered" by a script reader. The script reader has the job of reading the script and preparing an evaluation/grading of the script. This evaluation consists of a short synopsis of the story plus a brief grading and comments on:

➢ Is it well written?
➢ How interesting is the story?
➢ Are the characters engaging and relatable?
➢ Marketability/commerciality potential
➢ Grade – "pass" or "worth further consideration"

   If a pass then goodbye to that company; but, if a yes then the script will be read by other executives and further evaluation will occur. Either way the writer should try to get a copy of the coverage as it may provide useful constructive criticism.

SCRIPT SUBMISSIONS

10 Things you should know before submitting your script to film executives:

1) You only have one chance to create first impression.
2) Know what your film is and its genre and what other films it is like.
3) Make sure the script is correctly formatted.
4) Make sure it is the correct length.
5) Clarify the theme of the story.
6) Make it exciting, intriguing, and compelling.
7) Never have the villain reveal their plan.
8) Make sure every character has their own story to tell.
9) Don't give everything away.
10) Have a professional read it to get constructive feedback.

YOU WANT TO SELL THE SCRIPT TO A PRODUCER/DISTRIBUTOR

The reason for selling your script is hopefully to get the script turned into a feature film so that you and the kids can get the DVD or see it on TV! How do you do that? Now you can do this yourself or go sign an agent to represent you and your script, who can do it for you. Either way it is best to be able to pitch your idea/screenplay.

The Pitch - A pitch is a verbal presentation to an interested party that explains the story, the concept and its important elements. When I state an "interested party", I am referring to the fact you have the right person in front of you at the pitch that can move you forward in the process of selling the project. The mailroom person is probably not the right person! Try to ensure you are pitching to a development executive or acquisitions executive of a reputable film industry company or an agent you wish to sign with.

The dictionary definition of a pitch can be "a persuasive sales talk" or "attempting to sell/motivate in a high pressure manner". The object is to persuade the person listening to the pitch to buy into it. In the case of a film project idea the pitch can involve just the idea or concept or it can, of course, include a script attachment to assist in the presentation. In the case of just an idea or concept for a film being pitched, the idea is for the writer to persuade the listener (studio executive/acquisitions executive) to have them write the script based on the idea/vision given in the pitch. If the idea or concept is brilliant then the idea will be immediately taken up and the script written – but that does not happen to often!! The pitch of an idea has, therefore, to be inspirational and different. If you look at the concept of the successful film " Sideways" the pitch on this project could be that two middle aged guys take a trip to the wine country and find a couple of women and get drunk - not very inspirational! Or the pitch could be all about two guys and a journey of self-discovery – a much more marketable concept. So we are looking for a unique idea/concept that is marketable.

The following are six important points to assist you in your pitch of your unique and marketable idea/concept:

1) **Opening** - Always show interest in the person (and who he is) you are pitching to.

2) **Good Positive Energy** – Create a positive image and aura. Inspired delivery of the pitch – be expressive, animated and passionate during the pitch, but be controlled. Intrigue the listener so that they want to hear more.

3) **The Setup** – Explain briefly how your idea/concept came about. If applicable have props - a short 2 minute video, location photos or a story board. This helps transform your concept into reality.

4) **The Ending** – Make sure the idea has a positive and uplifting ending that is satisfying to the listener.
5) **Summary** – At the end make a short positive summary of the concept and why it is marketable. Always be careful of comparing your idea/concept with previous successful films of a similar genre or storyline – sometimes that helps and other times it might backfire.
6) **Collaborative Nature** – Highlight your desire to work in a collaborative manner with the group/company.

ACTORS, AGENTS, AND AGENCIES

Let us look into the delicate world of the relationship between independent film producers and the talent and those that represent them – the agent. Many people contribute to the making of a film – writers, directors, actors, cinematographers, composers, set designers, costume, editors, etc. All must work in harmony to produce the final product. Often the creative talent of writers, directors and actors are represented by agents.

A talent agent, or booking agent, is a person who finds jobs for actors, writers, musicians, producers, etc. in the film industry. Agents make their money by taking a percentage of the money that their client is paid.

Top talent agencies are:
➤ Creative Artists Agency (CAA)
➤ International Creative Management (ICM)
➤ United Talent Agency (UTA)
➤ William Morris Endeavor Entertainment (WME Entertainment)
➤ Agency for the Performing Arts (APA)

An agent provides essential services to their clients. This includes searching for and evaluating film prospects that their clients might work on. Plus, they will negotiate their fees and finalize the contracts. An agent represents their talent to the rest of the film industry. They are the guardians of their client's interests. An extensive list of agents and agencies representing talent can be found in the Hollywood Creative Directory – Representation (www.hcdonline.com).

Actors may be interested in working theatrically (stage, film or television) as well as in commercials. Some agents will handle all types of acting work while others specialize in a particular area. There are agents who represent television, voice-overs, or just film and television. Typically, the larger the agency, the more specialized the agents.

An agent has two sets of clients - the "talent" (actors, directors, writers, etc.) and the "buyer". The buyer can be a studio, casting director, advertising agency, production company or photographer.

Agents promote talent to the buyers, submitting talent that have the appropriate age, race, sex, look, talent, etc. that the buyer is seeking for their film project. Usually, an agent submits the actor's headshot or the director's credits to the buyer. After the buyer has made choices, the agent then arranges an audition or meeting. After the buyer has met the talent, the buyer will contact the agent if any of the talent will be hired. The agent will coordinate all the details of the assignment as well as negotiate the contract or pay.

The agent's job is to get the talent auditions/meetings with the right people who can hire them for a project. Agents take a 10 to 20% commission of the gross, depending if the job is union (such as SAG-AFTRA) or not. Union jobs are paid based on negotiated guidelines. Non-union is based on free open negotiations. A well-established agent will have networks upon networks of contacts in the film business.

The relationship between talent and a producer on a new project can be a delicate one. It is important to try and ensure the agent is always kept in the loop. An agent who is frustrated by your lack of professionalism can kill any future a producer may have with talent on your project.

When dealing with named talent the agent will usually request a formal offer be made for the talents' services (date, length, fee, etc.) and that the offer be backed by the financial means to pay that talent. In the low budget independent film business that can always create a problem as having money sitting in a bank account that can be verified by an agent can present difficulties. The producer should ensure they do all the necessary homework on the talent and that any offer is reasonable and based on industry standards. Any producer should be aware that an agent, especially in the larger agencies, can and is often, a valuable creative resource should they be brought into the project because they can package their agencies talent.

ACTORS - HOW TO GET AN AGENT

The wrong agent could harm your acting career!

There are all different kinds of agents. One of the most important differences is between franchised agents and non-franchised agents. Franchised agents are preferable. They are licensed to represent union performers - American Federation of Television and Radio Artists (AFTRA) and Screen Actors Guild (SAG) are two of the bigger unions. Please note - union actors also get better wages and better working conditions than non-union actors. To build an acting career it is best to be union. Before signing with any agent, call the SAG office to make sure that the agent is franchised.

What type of agent should you look for? There are different types of agents:

➢ Commercial agents handle commercials.

➢ Theatrical agents handle movies and television.

➢ Voice-over agents handle radio and other off-camera work.

➢ Modeling agents handle print and modeling work.

➢ Variety agents handle nightclub and personal appearance work.

➢ Full-service agents handle all types of work in all sectors.

Limited experience actors should try a commercial agent first to get some experience, or both a theatrical and a commercial agent, or a full-service agent who can handle television, movies and commercials. Commercial work will help to build the resume and earn you some nice fees. It's hard to find an agent so the best way to find a good one is to network and ask around.

Headshots are an important part of your marketing portfolio. Make sure you are working with a good photographer who is experienced in providing audition type headshots and make sure you get the negatives. If you are trying for different roles, you will need different photos for different looks you're portraying. Good professional headshots are a must.

The initial photos that will be sent to agents are 8x10 black-and-white headshots, with a line containing your name either in the lower left-hand border of the photo, or in the lower center border. Attached to the back of your photo is your resume. Keep the resume to one page and be clear on your experience in acting and not that you work at McDonalds! Your name goes at the top of the resume and any union affiliations. Contact details are next. Always ensure that you have your email account and phone number listed. Once you get an agent your contact details will be your agent's office address, phone and email.

List all your relevant credits. Try to ensure the most impressive are clearly noticeable. No age details are needed. Your education can help and having a good acting teacher or film school will also help. Also, include hobbies and useful skills.

Getting an agent is not easy. Being persistent is good - being a pest is bad. Every six weeks or so re-contact all the agents you have contacted by sending them a postcard-size headshot with your name, contact information and an update of what you've done recently. Organization helps in your pursuit of getting an agent.

One day – some agent will come calling so be prepared to meet with him and impress him with your talents and personality. Two or three monologues are a must. Be prepared to read a scene with someone at the meeting. Make sure you are dressed appropriately in decent casual smart clothes and well groomed. Be professional at all times. Trust your instincts and do due diligence on the agent that they are good and reputable.

Be careful never to sign anything without careful evaluation. Get advice. Exclusivity for two years with an agent means you are his – come good or bad so be careful who you sign with and for how long.

Warning! New talent is advised to research and find established agencies. No reputable agency charges for representation. However, the agent may recommend steps that will cost money, especially when talent is starting out. An agency may suggest new photos or training, and may have good contacts for new talent. An advantage of having an agent is that agents will help choose the best photographers or shots to make into headshots, etc.

Agent vs Manager

Agents have the authority to make deals for their clients. Managers establish connections with producers and studios, labels and publishers. They also guide the artist's career.

LOW BUDGET INDEPENDENT FILM SUCCESSES

"Clerks" - Kevin Smith, wrote, directed, produced and acted in Clerks. Smith provided a quality script that was shot on a $27,575 budget. Smith filmed almost the entirety of his film in the convenience store where he worked. Smith was only allowed to film at night while the store was closed (from 10:30 p.m. to 5:30 a.m.). To simulate day scenes while it was still dark outside, Smith had someone jam gum in the padlocks of the steel shutters, keeping them closed hiding the night sky from the audience. The film grossed over $3 million in theaters, with millions more by way of VHS and DVD sales.

"Blair Witch" - Daniel Myrick and Eduardo Sanchez, who co-wrote and co-directed The Blair Witch Project put together an original script and played a vital role in managing and directing the creative elements that made their film successful. They used unconventional methods to keep the film looking like as much like a documentary as possible. Such antics included the use of local mythology to capture reaction from real locals in the town where filming was done, and where the supposedly "real" events took place. The directors also allowed the "actors" to operate the camera, as they would in an authentic documentary. They cast actors who had no real acting experience, and in so doing, they created a sense of realism, as the film was portrayed as a documentary.

The Blair Witch Project is a great example of highly effective and original marketing. Production costs were low (approx. $25,000) and an additional estimate of $500,000 to $750,000 was added by Artisan, the distributor. The true success of Blair was the marketing prepared and executed by the directors. The film's buzz was largely generated by a website that was created a year before the film was even released. Launched in June 1998, they pretended the story was real and added outtakes from "discovered" film reels. They also posted fake historical text and police reports. The website had weekly updates, new information from the story added more interest. The website was an entertainment experience in itself. Instead of broadcasting to the passive masses, it targeted a "small, rabid and influential clique that might seek out a witchy internet site". Results - fans set up hypertext links between various sites, as well as to other film or occult sites. The Independent Film Channel aired "Split Screen" program - a short documentary spot of Blair Witch to generate interest. This show gave an inside look on independent moviemaking.

John Hegeman and Gary Rubin, Artisan marketing heads (Artisan saw the film at Sundance Film festival and bought it for $1m), contributed $15 million for marketing and distribution. They wanted to remain below the radar so it wouldn't register as hype. The campaign included tie-ins for books and TV specials, blitz campaigns on college campuses and commercial merchandise, including a soundtrack CD. The end result was a film that grossed over $248 million worldwide with millions more from DVD and TV.

"Paranormal Activity" - DreamWorks picked up the film for $500,000. Shot in 2007, it is a supernatural thriller about a young couple who experience spiritual possession. Shot mostly with a camcorder in a documentary style with a budget of only $15,000.

The film is truly marketed 'for the people by the people' utilizing a clever internet marketing campaign. The film first screened in college towns with its viewers heading to Twitter. Released only on YouTube, it found over a 1+ million views. Its trailer is simple yet effective as is the film.

According to trade magazine, Variety, the film earned $7.1 million over its first weekend of release. The director, Oren Peli, first showed his film at the Slamdance Film festival in 2007, though its distribution release was delayed until 2009 when Paramount picked it up for international release. The film was released to US audiences to a major success.

What makes Paranormal such a great film case study is that it is similar to Blair Witch. It's well-made and it used guerrilla style marketing to feed its enormous success. Using YouTube, word of mouth, internet buzz and other low-budget marketing approaches to gain hype and commercial success, Paranormal is a real example on how a small film can turn into something bigger than anyone could have ever thought.

10 THINGS THAT HOLLYWOOD DOESN'T WANT YOU TO KNOW!

These things will help you navigate the dark and sinister corridors of Hollywood. To deal with agents or executives like the "Entourage" agent character of Ari Gold or deal with the lonely trudge of getting an audition or the frustration of getting close to financing your small film but something goes wrong - these little "things" will help guide you. BUT, the most important fact for anyone entering the film industry is to know your craft. That means that if you are a wannabe filmmaker you must read and study all you can find about filmmaking; an actor needs to go to classes, practice and read up; a cinematographer needs to do the same. Know your craft, whatever that is!

#1) Always be professional and remember "first impressions"
Be professional both in your look, and also in your manner and attitude. A pointer that needs to be thought about includes your address! Yes your address should be in a "good" area of Los Angeles such as Beverly Hills or Santa Monica, Brentwood – go get a PO Box and give a right impression.

Another pointer concerns your telephone number – try and get one in Los Angeles area and not your old home number from Boise, Idaho. Shows you are in the LA area and not trying from the middle of the US.

LA is all about impression. Therefore, fitting in and giving the right impression is very important. I remember talking to a young budding actress who had made a couple of commercials and had just gotten a small supporting role for one episode in NYPD Blue. She decided to buy a BMW as that will provide her the right successful image when going to auditions, meeting executives, etc. What she doesn't tell anyone was that the car payment was so large she moved out of her single apartment and moved into another apartment she shared with two other people, to help reduce her apartment costs so she could ride around in an expensive car – all for impression and image!

Now we get to an important pointer that addresses where you actually live while trying to get in to Hollywood. It is very, very difficult to make headway with your career if you live in the middle of the US when the business is in Los Angeles – you make the decision on this!

Always be polite and well-mannered no matter what – you never know who you are talking to!

#2) "It's not what you know, it's who you know"

Hollywood is a town built on relationships. Make friends yes, but make the right kind of friends that will help your film career. The pyramid effect is an important element in. You will never get anywhere sitting in your lonely apartment waiting to be discovered. Similarly, you will get nowhere if all your friends are in the same boat as you – sitting in coffee shop all day complaining about how hard it is to get that break! You need to find the right type of friends – those that can benefit you.

Some of the ways include joining film communities/organizations such as Women in Film. There are lots of "meetup" communities, plus go to classes for your craft, UCLA extension classes and expand your network of contacts. Over time your network will expand. Make sure you focus of the right people and not just people who you think you might get a "date" with. Although that is important, it will probably not do a lot of good for your film career.

Parties, parties, parties (especially wrap parties or film premier parties) – they are always great places to meet people. Try and get invited to industry parties. Learn how to ask the right questions to find out who can be helpful and who is in the same boat as you – sounds selfish - but this is business so do what you need to do. Another tip is never get drunk or over drink at industry parties – you never know who sees you being an idiot.

The bottom line is that if you know someone who is connected to a film production or a sales agent or director it is often easier to do two things – one, is to know when films are coming up for production and two, there is more chance to be hired on the film in some capacity. So it helps to know the right type of people!

#3) "Know when to shut up and know your stuff"

So many people who want to be in the film business show their ignorance by not fully understanding the film business and not even fully understanding their own area of interest. Hollywood is full of wannabe "producers". I have been in so many meetings with such people who just talk and talk - but what they are saying is not said professionally and they do not use film industry terminology correctly or not at all.

Know your business and know the film industry terminology and when to use it. Less is more sometimes. I remember one producer was talking to an investor on a film project and did a great job. The investor basically agreed to fund his movie but the producer did not stop talking. He had the deal done but just kept talking until he talked himself out of the deal. The investor just got up and walked off because the producer just could not shut up!

Often I can make a determination on whether a person understands my business after just a couple of minutes talking to them. Their phraseology and how they put sentences together and use film terms is a dead giveaway. So know your stuff and know when to shut up!

#4) "If they want that – give 'em that - but?"

What do I mean by this? I remember a writer/producer coming to me and telling me that it is time for his script/his project to be the next hit genre. I, of course, was intrigued to see this new genre and was presented with "black gay romantic comedies". He could sell this all across the USA and make tons of money internationally – his words. Ok! – I know industry executives constantly talk about wanting material to be "different", "fresh", "original" – but they only mean that up to a point. So let's not get carried away. If a film executive asks for "x" or "y" then give him that. Do not try to re-invent the wheel. While creativity within a genre or writing style will always be encouraged - listen to what the film executive or producer or sales agent or investor wants. A writer coming to a producer with a new genre "black, gay romantic comedies" might not get the response they are looking for. But, if they come with a new fresh approach to an action genre film like Quinton Tarantino's "Kill Bill" or the approach taken on the "SAW" horror films, then originality wins through.

Be careful not to jump on to a trend that has been going for some time. It will end before you get on the band wagon and you will fail. A great example of that was the "Die Hard" trend of "man vs master criminal" films.

How do you choose what to write or direct or produce? This is a great question as there is always this temptation to follow trends even though they might not suit your style or preference. Therefore, always be honest to yourself, as the amount of time and effort will be great so make sure you are committed to the project. To help in this aspect, first identify the type of films and TV shows you prefer and the stories they project – the genre. Once you have a genre in mind, bring a new focus, something different to the project. Finally, try and stay ahead of the curve and of trends.

Remember, everything old is new again! How often have I heard the "meet" phenomenon? The "meet" is a film industry shorthand to illustrate an idea for a film project - namely, "Ghostbusters meets E.T. = Men in Black" or "Alien meet Predator =?", "Love Story meets Vampires = Twilight". The film industry will always look for sure bets and sequels are a common avenue for film executives. Of course, in recent years having a comic book super hero has been a good route to follow. – Spiderman, Iron Man, etc.

Remakes of past hit films are another avenue thought to be a way to protect the downside. When presenting ideas it is important to provide the listener or reader with enough substance to make a commitment to you so make sure you provide enough detail.

For example, for a writer, make sure you present your film idea with substance:

- *Story Structure* – Act one is the set up; act two is the growing conflict; act three is the climax/resolution.
- *Character Arc* – Lead character must have a definitive arc - eg. from being down to good.
- *Theme* – Film is described in human terms - eg. Forrest Gump – "life is like a box of chocolates".
- *Credibility* – is the story real and believable?

One area that is so important, especially if you are just entering the film industry is the need for passion. The film industry is an industry driven by emotion and not necessarily by ideas. Emotion and passion are a requirement for all people in this business. It can separate you from other people and give you that edge. Whether it is the emotion and passion generated by the Entourage character of Ari Gold or the passion exhibited by James Cameron on his Avatar quest – passion is found in all levels of the film business. Even after 30 years in the entertainment business, I still get excited and have a drive and passion for the business and look, I'm writing a book and doing film biz seminars to assist people in their film careers. The passion is still there.

#5) Talent rules, therefore agents rule

In Hollywood talent rules the nest. As agents control the talent, the agents rule also. To be successful in the film industry, one needs an agent whether you are a writer, actor, director or producer. Hollywood has created a series of barriers to protect their assets and agents are one of those lines of defense to their talent.

There are many types of agencies and it is up to the individual to do the necessary research to try and find the agency best suited for them. For instance, if you are a budding writer and you are looking for an agent, an approach could be to find a writer you admire (and like his style of writing) and then go to the WGA and ask for that writer's agent. Then you can send a letter with a work sample to that agent to see if he would be interested in you being a client. Don't forget that the Hollywood Creative Directories (www.hcdonline.com) are a valuable resource for all matters of representation.

#6) Keep in touch, but don't be a pain

Keep records, track meetings, calls, and follow ups. Be organized and methodical. Track industry functions (plus internet communities) and make efforts to attend any and all social functions that may have film contacts present. That includes going to the AFM (American Film Market) - even though you can only hang out in the lobby/bar area due to badge restriction. Also, go to film festivals. Contacts abound so be on alert. Don't be a pest in following up meetings or discussions, but weekly contacts about events or movements are reasonable.

#7) Some comical and common misunderstandings/terms in the film industry:

Script:

➤ It shows promise means it really stinks!
➤ It needs some honing means change everything.
➤ Try and punch it up means I have no idea what I want.
➤ It needs some polishing means change everything.
➤ It needs some streamlining means complete overhaul.

Job Descriptions:

➤ Actor means frustrated human being.
➤ Producer means frustrated writer.

- Agent means frustrated lawyer.
- Lawyer means frustrated producer.
- Writer means frustrated director.

How they say "no" - ways film executives say NO is...

- Don't call me I'll call you.
- That is quite good. Let me kick it around.
- I'll get right back to you.
- Call me back next week = Stay out of my life.

Film industry executives are careful who they say "no" to, as they may be the next Spielberg! *Please note*: "Yes" is when the money is in the bank and you are spending it!

Other pointers you need to learn are:

- Know the difference between arrogance and confidence.
- Be careful of those who keep telling you how honest they are.
- With producers always ask for film credit credentials (IMDB)... otherwise forget them.
- Be wary of agents or producers or anyone that asks you for money.
- Be careful about name dropping – they might be stood next to you!
- Do not pretend you know about something when you don't - eg. Talking about international distribution when you really don't know. You will be sorry.
- Don't forget your dreams... Never forget them.

#8) "Do Lunch"

One of the most important events in the film business and therefore in assisting your career is to "do lunch". Business lunches are where deals are made and careers elevated or vice versa. So many important transactions occur over lunch so doing lunch needs to be discussed. Some of the rules of "do lunch" are:

- Select a restaurant that is film industry acceptable and that you will see and be seen by industry people. Check on "hot" eatery lists.
- Show up on time and dressed appropriately for the surroundings.
- If you have a good car use valet – if not park round corner and walk.
- Select a table with a good view of the other tables and entrance.
- If you know people at other tables then acknowledge but do not visit their table unless...they can alter your world and know you reasonably well.

> Do not have too much to drink – keep composed.
> Careful what you eat – simple and not messy.
> Don't leave to go to bathroom at end of meal before bill arrives – why? – looks like you are dodging paying the bill.
> Learn how to schmooze (engage in pleasant small talk).

#9) Always have a project ready

"I have numerous projects in various stages of development" – these words are part of your bible that you carry with you all the time. Tell anyone who asks what you have available. This establishes you as a professional. These words are good if you are a director, producer, writer or actor. If possible, it is best to have a script or extended treatment ready in your hand especially for important meetings. That type of comment or request could lead to the chances of being able to move forward on a project right then and there. It is a real opportunity you need to capitalize on.

#10) Rejection

Who likes rejection of any sort, let alone when it is your career! In the film industry rejection just comes with the territory so get used to it. Use it as motivation and not a reason for despair. Whether you are a writer, actor, producer or director or crew, rejection is par for the course. It is true that something like 90% of all the money paid to actors goes to 2% of the SAG membership. Only a small percent of actors actually make a living doing their craft. Keep in mind that the big pay days of $15m to Angelina Jolie and the like, certainly skew the stats. Also remember that executives might not say "no" directly but use such phrases as "Don't call me, I'll call you" as they may want your next project so let's not upset you. Not getting a call back is evidence of a "no" – but, also remember that it only takes one "yes" and your world could change big time!

#11) Ask for everything, demand nothing

Sorry I lost count of the number of points – 11 not 10!

One day you will be a producer and your project will get a "yes"…So now what do you do in order to get the deal you are looking for? You ask for everything. Here are some things to go for…

> Ask for casting approval
> Ask for final cut

> Ask for % of gross or minimum net profit
> Ask for an industry standard credit
> Ask for a % of merchandising
> Ask for your own trailer

What goes hand in hand with asking for everything is the need to ensure any deal is put in writing and fully executed, even when dealing with friends. Secondly, always keep a well-organized and detailed paper trail of deals/contracts/discussions/points.

Note: 100% of no film is 100% of nothing! I have seen on numerous occasions people getting greedy to a point where the deal goes down the toilet. 20% of something is better than 100% of nothing. Another example is where a writer demands to be a first time director and that is usually not going to happen. So when the writer will not change their position - ultimately the deal collapses and no film is made. Be prepared to share the credit and the spoils – greed will kill the deal!

Finally, the last RULE of HOLLYWOOD...take the money and RUN ...Don't walk!!

"HOLLYWOOD TALK" - GLOSSARY

Above-the-Line – Part of a film's budget that refers to the costs associated with major creative talent - the stars, the director, the producer(s), and the writer(s).

A-List – A Hollywood list of talent (actors, producers, writers, and directors) who are considered of the highest level and can, hopefully, ensure excellent audience response.

Attach – To get a commitment, either in writing or verbal, from an actor, writer, producer, director to work on a film.

B-List – A Hollywood list of talent (actors, producers, writers, and directors) that are considered second tier, whether on their way up or way down; or, those who haven't made the A-list yet.

Back-End – The money left over from a film's sales after all costs have been accounted for.

Below-the-Line – Part of a film's budget that refers to the costs associated with the technical aspects of the film, including the crew, editing, sound, camera, etc.

Business, the – Term identifying the film and television industry.

Buzz – A film's perceived reputation before, during and after its release.

Chick Flick – A film identified to attract mainly a female audience.

Coverage – A short written report which evaluates the commercial attractiveness of a script. It can also be used regarding the adequacy of camera takes in a scene.

Development – Generic term regarding the writing and rewriting a screenplay. Development hell is the state of endless rewriting.

Do Lunch – A common Hollywood term for entertainment people to discuss business at lunch.

Franchise – A series of films based on an original hit.

Genre – A category or type of subject applicable to a script/story. Action or romantic comedy are examples.

Greenlight – A film can now go into production.

Gross – Total amount of box office receipts.

Legs – A film's ability to maintain, over a period, a high level of box office receipts.

Logline – A short, one or two sentence description of what the film is about.

One-Sheet – The poster of the movie.

Package – A collection of important elements of the film – such as writer, actor, director.

Pass – Rejection.

Post-Production – Film is edited, has music, has sound effect, etc.

Pre-Production – Process of getting the film ready to go into production.

Production – The actual shooting of the film.

Property – The underlying basis of a film project is the screenplay or book.

Schmooze – Indulging in pleasant small talk prior to getting down to business.

Shop – To shop means to try to sell your project.

Spec – Usually refers to a script that has been written without a commitment to be produced.

Tank – To die!! Film does very badly at the box office.

Tentpole – A major event movie that is a studio's flagship release.

Trades – Entertainment industry newspapers – eg. *The Hollywood Reporter.*

Wrap – The act of finishing a film shoot or the end principal photography.

****

ACKNOWLEDGEMENTS

Over the thirty years or so I have been involved in the film industry, the larger part of which has been in the independent film business, I have learnt much from many people, events, situations and, of course, from producing, financing, marketing, distributing and selling hundreds of independent films both in the USA and internationally. Also, during my career in teaching at major US universities my absorption of information has been enormous. I have talked to many very smart and knowledgeable people in the film business and read hundreds of articles, case studies, books, internet blogs, internet articles and trade papers - far too many to mention. Over the last three years, I feel I have read every book available to me on the independent film industry concerning the business aspects - again too many to mention. All these sources have contributed to my knowledge of this business. My own experiences and day to day film business involvement over these many years has also provided me a huge reservoir of knowledge. The combination of all these sources has contributed to this book and I would like to thank all of them.

I list many of these sources below and I am sure I have omitted some....please forgive me.

Hollywood Reporter- www.hollywoodreporter.com

Variety – www.variety.com

Screen International - www.screendaily.com

The Business of Film- www.thebusinessoffilm.com

Backstage - www.backstage.com

Videomaker – www.videomaker.com

DV magazine – www.mydvmag.com

MovieMaker – www.moviemaker.com

Studentfilmakers mag – www.studentfilmmakers.com

Writers / Storyboard Software - WritersStore.com

Filmmaking Contracts - FilmTvContracts.com

Software - Media-Services.com

Budgeting Software - ShowBizSoftware.com

Movie Scheduling Programs - ShowBizSoftware.com

Moviemaking Magazine - Moviemaker.com

Filmmaking info - Filmmaking.net

Independent Filmmaker - Filmmaker.com

Filmmaking Encyclopedia - Filmunderground.com
Film Production News - StudioDaily.com/fillmandvideo
Film Editing News - PostMagazine.com
Filmmaking Magazine - FilmmakerMagazine.com
Shooting People - www.shootingpeople.org
Hollywood Screenwriter - www.hollywoodScriptwriter.com
Writing Movies / Business of Screenwriting - www.ScreenTalk.Biz
Screenwriter Magazine - www.ScreenwriterMagazine.com
Online Writers Magazine / Screenwriter Basics -
www.ScreenwritersUtopia.com
Register Screenplay / Writers Guild Magazine - www.WGA.org
Script News / Selling Scripts - www.ScriptMag.com
Screenwriting Tricks / Screenwriting A-Z -
www.CreativeScreenwriting.com
Screenwriting - www.ScreenTalk.org
Screenwriting Software - www.WritersStore.com
Screenplay Resources - www.SFinaldraft.com
Screenwriter Resources - www.ShowBizSoftware.com
Copyright a Script - www.LOC.gov
Sell a Script - www.HollywoodLitSales.com
Screenplay Pitches - www.ScriptShark.com
Script Sales - www.ScriptPipeline.com
Selling Pitches - www.MoviePitch.com
Buying scripts - www.ScriptSales.com
Movie Scheduling - MindStarProds.com
Shooting Schedules - EntertainmentPartners.com
Budget & Schedule Software - ShowBizSoftware.com
Filmmaker Tools - FilmmakerTools.com
Budget - Movie - FilmBudget.com
Budget Software - Easy-Budget.com
Filmmaker Budgets - BoilerPlate.net
Independent Film Budgets - JungleSoftware.com
Actors Resources - ActorSource.com
Actors Chatroom - ActorSite.com
Actors Career Guidance - StarvingActor.com
Film Actor Monologues - ActorPoint.com
Film Acting Monologues - ActorTips.com

Screen Actor Craft - ActorsCraft.com
Acting on the Web - ActingOnTheWeb.com
Acting Business - ActingBiz.com
Actors Directory - HCDonline.com
Movie Actor Resumes - ActingResume.com
Film Casting - BreakdownServices.com
DV Magazine / DV Information - DV.com
Digital Videomaker - Videomaker.com
Digital Producer – DigitalProducer.Digitalmedianet.com
Digital Film Information - DVinfo.net
RES Magazine - RES.com
Backstage Mag.
Digital Videography - Videography.com
Digital Movie News - DVcentral.org
Film Festival Directory - FilmFestivals.com
Film Festival Promo Site - FilmThreat.com
Film Festival Database - FilmFestivalSource.com
Film Festival Lists - InsideFilm.com
Film Festival Submissions - WithoutaBox.com
Cannes Film Festival
AFMA Independent Film and Television Alliance
Raindance Festival

Paul Lazarus * Stacey Parks * Dov Siemens * Jason Brubaker
Sheri Candler * Jim Marrinan Steve Blum * Jason Squire
Robert Marich * Adam Davies * Nicole Wistreich * Renee Harmon
Phil Hall * Jeffrey Ulin * Reed Martin * Harris Tulchin * Mark Litwak
Mark Halloran * Gunnar Erickson * Schuyler Moore * Tiiu Lukk
Jay Conrad Levinson * John L Lee * Rob Holt
Louise Levison * Harold Vogel * Paul White

****

INDEX

Made in the USA
Lexington, KY
27 August 2011